T0063011

DREAMS
and
VISIONS:

VOLUME 1:

*The Expressed, Inspired,
Secret, Revelations: of God:*

Apostolic Mandate

CHRISTOPHER COVINGTON

BALBOA.
PRESS
A DIVISION OF HAY HOUSE

Unless otherwise indicated, all scriptures are
taken from the KJV of the Holy Bible.

Balboa Press books may be ordered through booksellers or by contacting:

Balboa Press
A Division of Hay House
1663 Liberty Drive
Bloomington, IN 47403
www.balboapress.com
1 (877) 407-4847

Printed in the United States of America.

ISBN: 978-1-4525-1553-3 (sc)
ISBN: 978-1-4525-1554-0 (e)

Balboa Press rev. date: 08/18/2014

Contents

Preface

D o you dare to dream? Do you desire to become something? Well do you know that there is inside of you in the bio spheric metric of your mind hidden treasures of wealth and hidden secret of God waiting to come forth? You are a direct product of the dreams and visions that are Inside of you. Whether it is something about your past, present, or future this book will explain to you the direct order and operations of the destiny code that is in you waiting to be birthed forth out of you. In this book Apostle Christopher Covington will teach and explain to you the order and operation of dreams and visions. Because you can understand these treasures that are given to you from God.

Introduction

And he said, Hear now my words if there be a prophet among you, I the Lord will make myself known unto him in a vision, and will speak unto him in a dream. Numbers 12: 6: Dreams and Visions have been hidden, as a form or something scary that mans' system has portrayed, as foolish which in actuality is deception of the devil. Because when they knew God, they glorified him not as God, neither were they thankful; but became vain in their imaginations, and their foolish hearts was darkened. Professing themselves to be wise they became foolish. Who changed the glory of the incorruptible God into an image made like to corruptible man and to birds, and to four-footed beasts, and creeping things. Romans 1: 21-23. Dreams and visions should not scare you. They are given to us from God through his Holy Spirit to show and reveal unto you the Expressed, inspired, secret, revelations of God concerning His only begotten son.

Dedication

I dedicate this book to Bishop Anthony A. Allen of Anthony Allen Ministries. www.allenent.org He is my big brother in the Lord. He has mentored and pushed me into the things of God. I dedicate this book unto Pastor Christine Allen who is my Mother in the Lord. She has contributed a lot into my growth and development in knowing God as well. Pastor Christine as a pastor operates strongly as a teacher in the word of God. I also want to acknowledge my wife Jade Covington who has stood by me from the beginning. I dedicate this book unto my brother Minister Marcus Covington who is a scholar in the word of God. He has been very faithful unto God. Another strong person I'd like to mention is Pastor John Paul Jackson of streams ministries. I saw him on the Joni show in 2004 and the topic was on dreams and visions. As he was speaking my faith ignited to a very high level, and he was being asked questions concerning dreams, and visions and he answered them well. He also interpreted peoples' dreams and visions and the Holy Spirit spoke to me and told me that just like John Paul Jackson interprets dreams and visions so can I. And greater works shall I do. And I also was motivated to write this book because of the Master Prophet Bishop E. Bernard Jordan of Zoe Ministries in which he uses as his motto destiny is not left up to Chance but it is a matter of choice. And the Holy Spirit spoke to me as I saw him on TV late night and told me that just like Bishop Jordan prophesies so can I and greater works shall I do.

Chapter 1

Dreams and Visions

There is nothing that can change you, your situations, nor circumstances without God revealing unto you who you are in him. This is a first step to the process to the seed which he has given you through dreams and visions. The question is that comes to mind is do you have dreams and visions? Which the answer would be yes? Don't let them scare you because it is a methodical processing system that God uses to make us inquisitive so that we can know that there is more to the outside realm that we occupy which is called space and to know that there are worlds all around us invisible and visible. There are worlds here on earth. There are worlds in the second heaven known as outer space but we know it to be as the second heaven. So then if there are natural worlds which are composed of substances which formulates into the correct terminology known as spheres. Then beyond a shadow of a doubt there is a world inside of you that's revealing who you truly are and the potential that you have. And the reason why you have not moved beyond the matrix of the physical

1

reality is because you haven't tapped into your mirror image which is your true divine nature of I am. You can either believe in what you see in the natural or in the spirit. The natural man cannot perceive the things of the spirit because they are foolishness unto him. They are spiritually discerned. The seer which is a person who sees in the spirit realm in a higher frequency than a prophet connects both the natural and spiritual world together to make sense of the chaos going on in your life. To give you peace and confirmation. The word seer is to see and the letter r is revelation that a person who sees into the spirit. A prophet speaks more than a seer. A seer sees more than a prophet. If one is called into the Apostleship he or she must first go through the metamorphical changes of a prophet then to an apostle. I have a yahoo group on yahoo.com called larva ignition of the butterfly effect which is a group about the adolescences of mankind unto the full maturity of that person. There must be an order into the things of God whether you are a born again believer or a person who has not received Jesus Christ in your heart as your personal Lord and savior that to the intent that you may know that this is for all cultures, backgrounds, ethnics, or moral beliefs. This book is a must to discover the explorations of the similitudes of the dark speeches of God. Dreams and visions have been lying dormant in people based on bias and ignorance. And that there are wells of hidden treasure and wealth in you that makes you up as a part of your genetic D.N.A. code that foresees the natural. Because what is natural? Its' called nature and natural is that which is known which we call fact. That which we as humans are accustomed unto that which is natural. We as believers in Jesus Christ know fact to be nonexistent for a short period of time because the spirit of God is truth which the truth overtakes the facts. Facts are the visible and the truth is the invisible realm. Everything that is made visible and invisible was made by the spirit of God. Things that we see were made by the spirit known as the invisible realm. That's why we as born again believers are supposed to call those things which be not as though they are. But that which is not natural is known as phenomenal or Spirit because the spirit never really makes sense. Stay away from people who do not understand you. Nine times out of ten they will hinder you from fulfilling the destiny call that is upon your life. Hang with and around those who understand you and where you are going. God will let you know who to allow into your life and who not to allow into your destiny. God just wants us to trust him even if we can't see it. In essence just as God told the Prophet Jeremiah in the book of Jeremiah Chapter 1: verse 5: Before I formed thee in the belly I knew thee; and before thou came out of the womb I sanctified thee, and I ordained thee a prophet unto the nations. Which God basically says that before any of us were ever formed in our mother's belly he knew who we were going to be before we ever came here on this earth. Jesus says in the book of Revelation Chapter 1: verse 8: I am the alpha and the omega, the beginning and the ending, saith the Lord which was, and which is to come the almighty. So in comparison he says that he knows the end from the beginning. That's why in dreams and visions he reveals to mankind pictures, symbols, and images that are based on mankind's level of understanding. When God begins to show and reveal to you these symbols of dreams and visions then we should know that they are parts of who he is. The creation in Genesis Chapter 1 verse 1 in the beginning God created the heaven and the earth. Earth is considered to be symbolic of your consciousness and heaven is considered to be symbolic of your subconscious. How can two walk together unless they be agreed? Isaiah 55:8-11 which are parables dark saying, and proverbs. God coming down to our level, dimension, or sphere to get our attention unto what He is really saying. God is speaking all the time but are we listening? Hearing is when it goes in one ear and comes out the other ear with no understanding. I use to hear that saying all the time. Listening is when you comprehend and understand what is being said at that time, to be used and applied for your life journey. For what you do at that time determines what time will give back unto you in time. Time is very precious and very valuable. For whosoever hears' which means listens shall more be given unto him because part of the manifestation comes in getting a full understanding of what you have listened unto. And that God did say that in the last days that he would pour out his spirit upon all flesh. Joel 2: 28; Acts 2:17. And the old men would see dreams and the young men shall see visions. So the order and operations of Dreams and visions are given to us through his Holy Spirit by his divine order. One of his operations among many is to pour out his character, nature, and divine will on mankind. We are going to talk about the trinity which is composed of God the father, God the son, and God the Holy Ghost, but that's another book that connects them, as one meaning Trinity or three. And yet God is the God head of them all, even though the word trinity is not mentioned in the bible it is a divine revelation from God, as many mysteries are not in the bible. The mysteries are given to us by God's spirit as we seek him in spirit and in truth. This brings us to a point issue of the dark forces or powers which is the Devil or otherwise known as satan the deceiver. A lot of people say that they had a bad dream which a lot of times is a device mechanism used by the devil to bring forth fear to hinder a person from the true reality of what God is trying to say, do and reveal unto them. And what is fear? I heard Kenneth Copeland say on the Believers Voice of Victory Broadcast that fear is having faith in death. So fear is opposite of faith. Faith comes by hearing and hearing by the word of God. It's time for people to come to the true knowledge of dreams and visions. Knowledge is a tree and that a tree produces forth fruit that has a quality taste that you would like, because of your free will to choose based on your desire to indulge the best. I use this example as an illustration to explain to you that dreams and visions produces fruit because of the type of tree it is. And that before you dream or envision a vision it starts off as a seed or the embryo that grows as you walk by faith. You must believe in your inner eye (realm of the spirit) or you will believe in your outer eye (what you see in the natural). Jesus says in the book of Matthew Chapter 7: verse 15: beware of false prophets, which come to you in sheep's clothing, but inwardly they are ravening wolves. False is opposite of real. And the only real thing is the truth. A Prophet is a spokesman of the Lord a divine messenger with a message from God. They protect the sheep from the wolves. They must listen to the Voice of the Lord and declare thus saith the Lord unto Gods people. Before we watch and guard ourselves from people who are false we must beware and watch out for the false prophets, otherwise known as evil and negative imaginations. They are projected thoughts that are vibrating into our minds that we allow to enter in unawares. They are known as Invisible spirits in the unseen world. Yes I said it. Not all imaginations are evil and negative. We must guard our hearts with all diligence as the scripture saith for out of our hearts flow the Issues of life. What are we seeing? What are we hearing? You are what you see. You are what you hear. You are what you allow to enter into your life. It can be based on ignorance or stupidity. Our emotions can play very important roles in the spiritual realm. Our emotions can be revealed in dreams and visions also. You can either control your emotions by prayer and discipline or let your emotions control you. For example a girl may have had a dream that she's falling and tripping on some concrete floor that's moving. And there are wolves coming after her.

And she sees an Angel in front of her dressed in white. And the wolves can't get to her but they're constantly moving in the same spot. And the Angel has his hands out for her to come to him but she's afraid. And the Lord could be telling her that her foundation which represents her faith is not solid, nor firm, because she allows her environment, based on her physical circumstances to dictate her life by causing her to fear. While the Lord has his hands out trying to tell her that she's not alone and that she need to keep her eyes on him. We as born again believers must know that there will be trials and tribulations. Remember that the devil can work in your 5 senses. What you see. What you hear. What you taste. What you touch. And what you smell. But the devil cannot manifest in the Truth because Satan is the father of all lies. The devil can operate and manifest in darkness to try and deceive people, but the spirit realm belongs to God. The devil can only operate in your life if you allow him too. Satan also can operate in your life whenever God permits him too. John 16:11. The reason why God threw Satan here on the earth is because the earth was a realm for him to rule in before he fell from grace. Remember the gifting and the callings of God are without repentance. Satan was supposed to lead the Angels and the human-race to worship God. So plans change but the purpose will always remain the same. The dream was to let the girl know to be of good cheer for He has overcome the world. The world is just a state of mind that is constantly changing because of its birth pains. That's why the bible tells us that in the book of Romans Chapter 12: verses 1-3 for us to be transformed by the renewing of our minds. Can I tell you that God is a transformer? Our God is a metamorphical God. He can change and shift into anything, anywhere, at anytime. Our God is awesome. He is the supreme, divine, ruler, of the universe. All dreams and visions are mirror images of what we are not aware of at a certain point in time. The word (of) is a place of location that can be identified, which is a pronoun whether it be past, present, or future. If you have a lack of vision then check your provision. The prophetic word is a gift of revelation enabling you to walk into the fullness of Gods destiny for your life. The prophetic word speaks death to your past but speaks life to your future. You are what you see that can determine your self esteem. It can demote you or promote you. What do you see? Do you believe what man tells you that you cannot do, cannot have, nor be? Or do you see and believe in who God says you are? You can do and be all that God has for you? It's all a choice. We must know we are God which is spirit. We have, possess, and walk in Gods divine nature. Do you understand what you see? Can you become what you see which is your desire? Do not accept roles that someone is trying to place on you to control, use, manipulate, and to victimize you. This type of psychology is known, as witchcraft. When someone uses control against another it is known as witchcraft.

You as a born again believer can avoid the weapons of the devil. Remember the weapons will form, but they will not prosper. These questions are only a sum of the quantity of the questions concerning the subject matter. There are many levels and dimensions of dreams that produce visions. Dreams and visions are in comparison the same. Dreams are known in the book of Numbers Chapter 12: verse 6 as God speaking to us and in verse 8 God uses the word dark speeches. We can formulate or compose that dreams is God trying to talk to us through puzzles, or riddles. Puzzles and riddles are known as parables, proverbs, and dark speeches. He says in verse 6 that he makes himself known to us in visions. Yes God makes himself known to us in visions. And just because God reveals himself to you in a vision doesn't make you a prophet. You can desire to be a prophet and God will grant your request. But be careful what you ask God for because there is a price for whatsoever you ask him for. Furthermore In verse 8 he says that Moses can see the similitude or image of the Lord. Even though in verse 6: God was describing the spiritual gifts of a prophet, or also known as a seer. This is only the beginning to the frontier of the mysteries of the Kingdom of God. We are going to tap into and discover more hidden truths of dreams and visions. We haven't even come close to the depthness of the spectrum that leaves us inquisitive with a lot of unanswered questions. This book is an intro to the many books that are going to be revealed in time to come. There are methods that you as an Individual must take in dealing with dreams and visions. First of all have a pen or pencil ready with a notepad. So when you wake up you can write down your dreams and visions in a dream journal. Be sure to write down the date of your dreams and visions. Put them in alphabetical order depending on how many you had that day. This will allow you to make a system that orders the events of your life that was revealed to you at a certain time. From my own personal experiences I started writing down my dreams and visions in a dream journal starting towards the end of 1999. And now I have at least 25 different thick journals of dreams and visions. A lot of my dreams and visions have come to pass. As an Apostle one of my spiritual gifts is dream and vision interpretation, as stated in the book of numbers Chapter 12: verse 6. Your dreams and visions should match up with the Word of God in the bible that should give you divine confirmation. Even though the dream or vision that you had looks like it matches up with the bible be very careful and seek the Lord for discernment, because satan is very busy trying to deceive the Saints of God. There are a lot of people who say that they are a prophet or a seer so be careful who you entertain. Not everyone who says that they are of God are from God. The proof is that Jesus said that you shall know the tree by its fruit. Matthew 7:20 Jesus also said that in the book of Matthew Chapter 24: verses 4-5 And Jesus answered and said unto them, Take heed that no man deceive you. 5. For many shall come in my name, saying, I am Christ; and shall deceive many. The Lord is telling us to be on watch because many people will be pretending to be of God. Many will say that they are from God but have motives from hell. Remember that God guides us by His Word, also as you develop a relationship with God through His Son Jesus Christ and the Holy Spirit you then begin to grow, develop, and mature in discernment. Knowing Gods Voice which Is His Word matures you to watch, listen, look, and to observe. The question is one that challenges you to do a self-analysis about where are you at in standing with God. If you are in right standing with God I challenge you to continue to seek the face of God to expand your tents for more and more of him. If you are not in right standing with God whatever level you are in your faith know that you can change by the power of God. If you are not saved or haven't received Jesus Christ as your personal Lord and savior this is your opportunity to do so. If you are serious and if you want to go to heaven one day then repeat this out loud and believe in your heart that God has raised Jesus from the dead. By making this conscious decision you can move forward in life. The bible says that in the book of Romans Chapter 10: verse 9: That if thou shalt confess with thou mouth the Lord Jesus, and shall believe in your thine heart that God has raised him from the dead, thou shalt be saved. Verse 10 says For with the heart man believeth unto righteousness; and with the mouth confession is made unto salvation. So beloved if you are a back slider or have never accepted Jesus Christ as your personal Lord and savior repeat this out loud from your heart. Believe that after you confess the sinners prayer that your life shall be instantly changed. Know that you destiny shall no longer be hell, but heaven and that you shall have God as your loving father. Dear Lord Jesus I am a sinner and I was born in sin and in sin did my mother conceive me. I believe that you died upon a cross for my sins, and I ask you to come into my heart and be the Lord and Savior of my life and I thank you. I ask you to give me the evidence of speaking in tongues and baptism of the Holy Ghost and fire and I thank you. Lead me to a home church where they are preaching and teaching the true gospel word. Give me pastors according unto your heart which shall feed me with knowledge and understanding and I thank you that my life is changed and that from this day forward I'll never be the same again.

I wrote this sinners prayer as I was led by the Holy Spirit because it will do you no good to read this subject matter about dreams and visions without having a relationship with God the father through Jesus Christ. The Holy Spirit will not reveal unto no one the answers or the interpretation of the word of God without having Jesus Christ as your Lord and Savior. The bible says that in the book of Jeremiah Chapter 33: verse 3: Call unto me, and I will answer thee, and show thee great and mighty things, which thou knowest not. The scripture is saying that he knows all things and he is also referred to as the revealer of secrets. The bible says that in the book of Ecclesiastes Chapter 5: verse 3: For a dream cometh through the multitude of business; and a fool's voice is known by the multitude of words. Dreams are building blocks, or puzzles that are for Gods work that he has for mankind to do. Genesis Chapter 1: verse 26: And God said, let us make man in our image, after our likeness: and let them have dominion over the fish of the sea, and over the fowl of the air, and over the cattle, and over all the earth, and over every creeping thing that creepeth upon the earth. The clearer revelation of dreams is the twin brother of the formulated entity known as a vision. A vision can be referred to as one with dreams. Dreams reveal riddles, puzzles, which are the dark speeches of God. To those who are neophytes visions are deeper visual revelations of God. The bible says that in the book of Matthew Chapter 5: verse 8: Blessed are the pure in heart: for they shall see God. They shall see the deep secrets of God through visual images. Research can be done as you go through the Holy Bible to see these subject matters used in historical peoples' lives that God used to talk too and to communicate with. 2 Peter 1: 21 For this prophecy came not in old time by the will of man: but holy men of God spake as they were moved by the Holy Ghost. That's why I say even on my blog talk radio shows and on talkshoe.com that every successful child of God must have a prayer life. This is a saying that I use a lot as I have heard preached time after time. Prayer is communication with God. The word communication is the word communion or commune which is to have fellowship with. We must know how to pray the biblical correct way on how to pray effectively so that we can get results. As

I was told in Sunday school years ago that no prayer no power more prayer more power. I used this term a lot in teaching Sunday school. So may born again believers say that they are Holy Ghost filled, but the majority of them have been in churches for decades and yet they cannot hear, nor discern the Lords' voice. For example; we can use the book of Revelation to see many visions that were given to the Apostle John the revelator on the Isle of Patmos. These visions that John saw are now being revealed unto the church past, present, and future of end time events. God uses vision in order for us to seek him for the revelation of the interpretation. God uses visions to reveal unto mankind what he is saying in a visual state. To test to see if the dream or vision is from God it has to match up with the word of God. The word of God should confirm what he has showed you. You should have peace about the dream or vision that you had. I said earlier that we must walk in discernment with razor sharp precision to determine if the dream or vision is from God. God will let us know if it's from him, as we seek him in prayer. You see every time I have a dream or vision God confirms the dream or vision by his word. I get confirmation from him because I know his voice. You also should know the voice of God. The spirit of God will tell me about the dream or vision therefore my joy and peace would increase. My faith in God would become ignited even the more. A fruit of the Holy Spirit is peace. Another fruit is joy. God confirms what he is saying a lot of times by parables, proverbs, the dark sayings of the wise, and by his word. God will use your pastor to confirm the word of the Lord. He will use Prophets to confirm his word also. Dreams and visions have warnings as, well as blessings. These are color schemes that are fluorescent and multi-faceted in essence. Remember again as you pray and seek the Lord he will give you discernment to see if the dream of visions is from him. Prophets are given the ability to interpret dreams. God will use not only prophets, but those who are willing and obedient. God is no respecter of persons. Prophets have dreams and visions, but prophets have more dreams than visions. Prophets speak more than seers. Now the Seer has dreams and visions but seers have more visions than dreams. You see before I became an Apostle I was a deacon for a few years then God elevated me unto Minister Christopher Covington. When it was time for my elevation God told me that I was an apostle. He told me that he was going to grow me through the metamorphical stages to manifest me as an apostle when it was time. So the Lord elevated me to a prophet in 2004 and in 2009 God told me that I was an apostle. The Apostle is a builder. They are wise master builders and operate in all the gifts of the Spirit. At times God uses me as a pastor, prophet, teacher, evangelist, and as an apostle. If you do not understand your dreams and visions go to your pastor and ask them to help you with the interpretation of your dream or vision. The first thing my pastor did at the time I told him that I saw a vision of me preaching the gospel he rejoiced, then told me to vacuum, clean the church and that he would be back. I heard Pastor Paula white give a testimony about when she told her pastor that she had a dream of her preaching in front of multitudes of people. She said that her pastor said great and gave her a broom to clean the church as well.

Key Point # 1:
We must humble ourselves under the mighty hand of God so that he may exalt us in due time.

I ministered on blogtalkradio.com and on talkshoe. com about the rise of power and I was ministering on the life story of Joseph; and one of my series scriptures was psalms 75: how it talks about God will humble the proud and boastful and will give grace unto the humble. If you do not understand your dream or vision go to a prophet because God says that in the book of Numbers Chapter 12: verse 6: And he said, Hear now my words: If there be a prophet among you, I the Lord will make myself known unto him in a vision, and will speak to him in a dream. The secret to verse 6: is that God makes himself known unto his seers in visions and will speak to his prophets in dreams. Prophets also can hear from God and also receive visions from God. A prophet mainly is going to hear from God and have a lot of dreams and fewer visions. Your seers are going to hear from God and have fewer dreams and more visions. These are gifts that a prophet has to help people to know and to understand what God is saying unto them. Prophets give directions and instructions unto people. Your divine purpose and direction is tied up in dreams and visions. You must know the voice of God which is the word of God in order for him to guide you and tell you what your dreams and visions are about. These are some of the basic foundational elements to the topic of our study so enjoy as we go to our next Chapter.

Chapter 2

Expressions: of God

An expression symbolizes someone or something that portrays the state of being. The state of being transforms to now which becomes alive. Hebrews Chapter 11: verse 1: says that Now faith is; so faith is now. An expression symbolizes someone or something that is a noun, and a noun is a person, place, thing, or ideal. The word ideal is a spirit. For God is a spirit, he is a transitional God, and he is a metamorphical God. Throughout the ages of the human race expressions were used, and are used even now to show a person's feeling vs. a thing which is inanimate that cannot show feelings. In psychology what the Lord has given me is a code that the flesh and soul is tied into the conscience which is the flesh side of man. Remember man is spirit. Man is male and female when we look at who we are in our true divinity. The Dominion Ship Creative Prophetic Healing Anointing is dominion ship. Remember Genesis Chapter 2: verse 7: And the Lord God formed man of the dust of the ground, and breathed into his nostrils the breathe of life; and man became a living soul. Man is spirit. Man is God in human form. If you do not know your true divinity then you are no different than an animal. The word struggle is false because the truth is that God has made us more than conquerors in Christ Jesus. Who is Christ Jesus? Jesus Christ is God in the flesh. People are judgmental because of ignorance or stupidity. Ignorant is when you don't know. Stupid is when you do know and do not care about the consequences. Don't argue with people about scripture, nor religion, nor about who you are, or what God has called and chosen for you to be and to do. Matthew Chapter 7: verse 6: Give not that which is holy unto the dogs, neither cast ye your pearls before swine, lest they trample them under their feet and turn again and rend you: In other words the devil don't know no more than what you tell him.

Key Point # 2:

Don't reveal nor share your knowledge, nor revelation with demons that's why Jesus said let the dead bury the dead. That brings me to our next point about our subject matter that expressions have symbols, known as signs that are a form or type of instrument to get a point across. Dreams and visions have symbols that makes up the formulate substance of the visual project. The bible says that in the book of Genesis Chapter 1: verses 1-2 that 1. In the beginning God created the heaven and the earth. 2: and the earth was without form, and void; and the darkness was upon the face of the deep. And the Spirit of God moved upon the face of the waters. It says that the earth was without form which says that there was no definite shape therefore the word without form was used as a word to describe something. To be without means lacking the manifestation of spirit. Everything comes from spirit which is mind. God thought it and his desire was so into being that it transformed into now present tense. The scripture says that it was void which indicates that it was empty. Being empty means not full. God comes to fill us or to make us full of him. Full of life, full of purpose, full of the essence of God. Symbols are used to express something that can describe the inanimate object, person, or ideal. It's all a noun. Noun is spirit. For example I like to rap because the Lord has called me into the arena of entertainment. In my rap music I like using signs with my body to express my emotions normally to add to my repertoire.

Key Point # 3:
You represent a symbol and your appearance reveals the type of signal that you are sending out into the world or universe.

The word universe is another terminology of the cycle of worlds combined into a whole. Existence is the universe incorporated with worlds. Your appearance comes from your state of mind which is your state of being. You can change your state of being by the renewing of your mind. For example, I always say that you can tell where a person is at by the expression on their face. Symbols are used in dreams to lead, guide, and direct, express, to reveal the instruction, directions, and the purpose of God for our lives based on the assignments that are given to us. I talked on blogtalkradio.com in 2011 which were my first messages on the science and art of creation about the universe. We must know that God speaks and reveals himself unto us by dreams and visions by invading our universe. Your universe is worlds that you possess and live in combined as a whole to create your state of being. This is also known as the universe. That's why when you are dealing with poor people you only give them one choice because they are stuck in a system and don't know how to get out. If they knew how to get out of their situation they wouldn't need one choice. They could decide on a better way to push themselves forward to success and achievement. That's why the rich make many choices and are not stuck in a system. The rich create systems for the poor. When you say that you are poor you lack imagination. This lack of imagination creates a lazy person. Who wants to be associated with lazy people? These are also false prophets that will try and infiltrate our minds if we are not watchful. This book that you are reading now is a system that God has given me to create. It's a blueprint given to me by God. When you do not make decisions and choices you are still a child. It takes maturity to break out of the system of poverty. When you make decisions and choices you are walking in your divinity even if you fail. The bible says that the righteous falleth seven times and get back up. You can check out my radio show on blocktalkradio.com at http://www.blogtalkradio.com/realmoftheseer. When the scribes and Pharisees asked Jesus to show them a sign or in other words they wanted proof of what he was saying. Jesus told them in the book of Matthew Chapter 12: verse 39: But he answered and said unto them, An evil and adulterous generation seeketh after a sign; and there shall no sign be given to it, but the sign of the prophet Jonas: now when you look at verse 39: in a dream you could picture wicked people committing adultery and doing what they chose to do. They knew the law and the 10 commandments were given to them as, well as unto the New Testament church. Even today the truth is given forth but we want to take prayer out of school because we try and justify our actions by saying that we can do what we want. Now our society especially in America is totally out of control. We must go back to the basics by having a prayer life. Even though we have a national day of prayer in the United States we must have a prayer life daily all the time. How much do you love someone that will cause you to give your life for them? I don't know too many people or even came across someone who would do that. Or how many parents would give their child up for someone else life? The answer is no one but God. John Chapter 3: verses 16-17 16. For God so loved the world, that he gave his only begotten son, that whosoever believeth in him should not perish, but have everlasting life. 17. For God sent not his son into the world to condemn the world; but that the world through him might be saved. This subject about love and especially verse 16: is considered to be some of the best scriptures in the bible. It expresses Gods love for sinners that it caused him to give the only thing which he loved the most which is his son Jesus Christ to redeem man from sin by his death. Therefore becoming sin that we may have eternal life. In the book of Jeremiah Chapter 29: verse 11: For I know the thoughts that if think towards you, saith the Lord, thoughts of peace, and not of evil, to give you an expected end. God's thoughts are expressed unto us of good, peace, and to give us an expected end. When God reveals to us dreams and visions he is expressing and revealing his love towards us. There are times that our bodies get real tired and we begin to nod off for a few seconds to a few minutes. In which your outward experience takes over and you are in another world. Your bodies are asleep in hibernation mode, but you which is spirit can see (seer) in another dimension or level beyond the natural realm. In other words you can see into the biospheric metric into the spirit. A lot of times God want to show and reveal to us things but we have so much junk going on all around us. So when our physical body goes into hibernation mode asleep we are present with the Lord.

Key Point # 4:
You never go to sleep. You are always awake at all times because you are God. Your physical body dies and goes into hibernation sleep mode while you are present with the Lord.

An example of key point # 4 is found in the book of Acts Chapter 10: verses 9-16: in which Peter went on top of a house top to pray and he became very hungry and would have eaten. But while they made ready he fell into a trance and as the story goes on God revealed unto Peter a vessel that was as by description a green sheet at the four corners and it came down to the earth. There were all types of beasts of the earth, creeping things, and fowls of the air. The Lord spoke to Peter and told him in verse 13: and there came a voice to him, rise, Peter; kill, and eat. And Peter told the Lord that he's not going to eat it. He told the Lord that he's never ate nothing common or unclean. The bible says that the Lord spoke to Peter the 2nd time and told him verse 15: and the voice spake unto him again the second time, what God hath cleansed, that call not thou common. Verse 16: this was done thrice: and the vessel was received up again into heaven. So God was trying to tell Peter in Chapter 10: of the book of Acts that he shouldn't be prejudice of the gentiles. God used the food to express or illustrate to him that those people that were coming to him were sent by him and accepted by him. Peter should have accepted them at the same time God was trying to relay and tell him that three times until Peter understood what he was saying unto him. The question that comes to mind is what expressions do you use? Sometimes we get happy, sad, discouraged, joyful, and excited. These are products of what we allow to enter into our lives and these things can change our countenance which alters our facial expression. I use this illustration dealing with expressions of the face to try to get you to understand that dreams and visions are expressions that portrays the character of God. The bible says that in the book of Jeremiah Chapter 29: verse 11: For I know the thoughts that if think towards you, saith the Lord, thoughts of peace, and not of evil, to give you an expected end.

Key Point # 5:
Can I tell you that Gods mind is full of you. Our God is the supreme, divine, ruler, of the universe. He is a telepathic God. God communicates with us through his word by his mind.

For example; by God displaying peace in his mind and not of evil manifests joy and happiness on his face. He says in verse 11: that he knows the thoughts that he thinks towards us. The word toward, towards, or the word to is a description of a place of location. A place of contact which if the place in which the thing is going or supposed to go does not have a name we call it space. We use proper nouns to describe important people, places, and things. Even ideals can become proper nouns if we label and make it as important. But we are all very valuable in the eye sight and mind of God. There are more examples of expressions that are used to show us about the subject matter in this chapter of the book you are reading now. Before we close with this chapter of expressions we can use for example the different types of dreams and visions that God gives to mankind to express his purpose for our lives. Dreams are more literal and visions are more pictorial. You can have day dreams, trances, spiritual visions, trans visions, and open visions. There are many more ways in which dreams and visions can be expressed.

Key point # 6:
The Holy Ghost has three types of visionary avenues to speak to us and that's dreams, visions, and trances.

The Lord has given me a (dream prayer) that you can use as a form of prayer to cause heaven here on earth into your life. Pray this prayer the dream prayer as soon as you wake up and go to sleep.

Dream Prayer: Father I thank you for revealing unto me in my dreams and visions the things that you desire for me to know and to resolve. Now the things that you desire to be canceled in my life let your spirit move upon those situations and let your power overshadow them and let them be canceled right now. Allow your word to be the ax in my life in Jesus name. And now for the things that you desire to come forth into my life let your spirit move upon these situations and let your power overshadow them and let them come forth right now in Jesus name. Give me spiritual- visions, trans-visions, and open-visions for your will, purpose, and assignment for my life. Give me the presence of mind of my angels. May I not be afraid of my angels. Give my angels the presence of mind of me and may my angels be not afraid of me. You said that you would guide me into all truth, bring all things back unto my remembrance, and show me things to come. So I receive your instruction and benefits for my life. Father cause those that you have assigned to be a blessing unto my life come forth into my life. Show and reveal unto me who they are. Show those that you have assigned to be a blessing unto me who I am. Confess my name unto them. Arise upon me Lord and cause your glory to daily be seen upon me. Cause the gentiles to come to my light and kings to the brightness of my rising. Cause my gates, doors to be open daily to cause people to give me the forces of the gentiles and that their kings may be brought. Cause them to acknowledge that you have loved me. Father use me to be a blessing unto your kingdom and use my gifts, talents, abilities, time, money and possessions to be a blessing unto those you desire. And I thank you that my thoughts and steps are established in Jesus name amen. Dreams mainly happen while you are asleep while your flesh is in hibernation. As I said before that you are never asleep for to absent from the body means to be present with the Lord. This means two things. Number 1: is when the Lord come and takes us into glory. Number 2: let's go to Jude verse 9: Yet Michael the archangel, when contending with the devil he disputed about the body of Moses, durst not bring against him a railing accusation, but said, The Lord rebuke thee. You see we shall now go into the metaphysics and science of this verse in the book of Jude. We are still on the subject matter of dreams at hand. Verse 9: shows us that Moses physical body had died. That's why in a funeral you hear the preacher always say ashes to ashes dust to dust which means that mans physical body goes back to the ground (earth) but your spirit never dies. Your spirit is forever eternally alive. So when Moses left his physical body satan came immediately to take Moses body but Michael the arch angel immediately showed up. You see angels can move at the speed of light. Here's the proof. Hebrews Chapter 4: verse 12: For the word of God is quick, and powerful, and sharper than any two-edged sword, piercing even to the dividing asunder of soul and spirit, and of the joints and marrow, and is a discerner of the thoughts and intents of the heart. Right here if we analyze Hebrews Chapter 4: verse 12: we see conclusively that angels are quick and sharper than any two-edged sword as the scripture further goes on. Lets' look at Psalm Chapter 91: verse 11: For he shall give his angels charge over thee, to keep thee in all thy ways. So we see here that the word angels is plural meaning more than one. If that is the case lets' look at Psalm Chapter 34: verse 7: The angel of the Lord encampeth round about them that fear him, and delivereth them. The word angel in Psalm Chapter 34: verse 7: is singular meaning one. So when we look back at Jude verse 9: we know that God shall give his angels charge over us and we see that the angel of the Lord encampeth round about them that fear him. God has given us multitudes of angels and as we pray angels are sent and released to go forth on our behalf. As stated in the book of Hebrews Chapter 1: verse 14: Are they not all ministering spirits, sent forth to minister for them who shall be heirs of salvation.

Key Point # 7:
Our angels are assigned to assist us in our purpose and vision that God has given us for our lives. Exodus Chapter 23: verse 20: Behold, I send an Angel before thee, to keep thee in the way, and to bring thee into the place which if have prepared.

As I said again that Exodus Chapter 23: verse 20: basically says that our angels are assigned from God to help and to assist us in our purpose and vision for our lives. If that's the case then the angel of the Lord as stated in the book of psalm Chapter 34: verse 7: is more powerful than all the other angels that God has assigned unto us. Psalm Chapter 91: 11: For he shall give his angels charge over us to keep us in all our ways. This brings me to this point. The angel of the Lord that is assigned to you is greater than all the other angels that are with you, because the other angels leave as we pray to God on our behalf and on others behalf's. The angel of the Lord never leaves us. So here's another point.

Key Point # 8:
We are daily having exorcism experiences. Whether we be saved or not saved, as we pray angels carry our words because we are brought with a price and angels move and hearken only to the word of God. It's not us,

it is the blood of Jesus Christ that he shed at Calvary's cross.

The word pray means speech or to speak. We must be very careful what we say because Proverbs Chapter 18: verse 21: Death and life are in the power of the tongue: and they that love it shall eat the fruit thereof. We have the uncanny supernatural enabling power to create our own destiny from fantasy, to reality, from fact unto truth. Daily we are having exorcism experiences. We are daily leaving our physical bodies and are being translated into realms and dimensions which is the spirit realm. This is known as the spirit world. That's why we must be very careful what we speak because whatsoever we say will take us there while we are not conscience of what we said. Remember that we cannot blame the devil for our reality because we created it. The church world says that the word exorcism is witchcraft but it's not witchcraft. It's witchcraft if you use anything,or serve anything as an idol or God; therefore you become disobedient and are seduced and enticed by your own lusts. Many times when we have dreams and visions we think that they shall happen in the future but in actuality they have already happened. The word exorcism means expulsion of an evil spirit, casting out of a demon. But that's the dictionary word definition of the meaning. The Lord told me that the word exorcism means to resurrect from the dead. Since our physical bodies are sinful they are considered dead. So it's our spirit that is alive and quickened because of Christ Jesus finished work at Calvary. That after his physical body died he descended into hell. His spirit went into the bowels of hell. He was having an exorcism experience. That's why he is the resurrection and the life the author and finisher of our faith. We are daily traveling and translating into realms and dimensions. I stated earlier that the word to is a word that means a place of location or destination. The mind is so powerful that we must be very careful what we say because a lot of times we become ignorant of the truth that we open doors that we don't even know about. That's why we shouldn't complain about the hell we are in because we created it. It's more to just your minds mind. It starts with your heart. Not your physical heart but your stomach area where the Holy Ghost Holy Spirit dwells and resides. If you're not saved you are demonically possessed and oppressed by demons. When you are saved you can no longer be possessed by a demon but you can be oppressed. That brings me to this point. Every time there is a move of God about to happen and is happening in your life we must be very careful who we talk too and associate with.

Key Point # 9:
The devil shall by the spirit of jezebel by demon demonic influence have many coming to us in Christ name saying they are the Christ. They are messengers of hell to derail, hinder, kill, steal, and destroy the dream, purpose, and assignment of God for your life. These are

31

known as destiny-killers, and dream-stoppers. These are jezebels-eunuchs.

These are satans' devices. I have seen the order and operation of satan many times. I have seen and still know a lot of people in the churches who say they are Christians who are working for the devil and don't even know that they are being used by him. I hear so many times and I know that you have heard this also. People say that they don't want to go to church because it's filled with hypocrites. Don't worry about the hypocrites. You must discern and know that you will either get training for your purpose and assignment for your life in church, the military, or in jail. You can have it the easy way or the hard way. I always hear that people in the church say they love me and we hear the song I love you. I need you to survive then a lot of them become envious of you. These workers of satan try and literally kill you. I have seen and have experienced attacks from people so many times that if am immune unto the attacks.

Key Point # 10:
God will isolate and hide you in a desert wilderness place for a times and seasons to protect you from the religious system of the devil which is jezebel. God does this so that we won't become contaminated with the religious system.

Isaiah Chapter 49: verse 8: Thus saith the Lord, in an acceptable time have if heard thee, and in a day of salvation have if helped thee: and I will preserve thee, and give thee for a covenant for the people, to establish the earth, to cause to inherit the desolate heritages. When God speaks to you mouth to mouth as stated in the book of Numbers Chapter 12: verse 6: he speaks to you literally. The word literally is an adjective. Literally means in a literal manner; accurately; actually; virtually mouth to mouth. To conclude the rest of this Chapter of dreams and visions it must match up with God's word which is the holy bible. God's word is his will and Gods will is his word. God, Jesus, and the Holy Spirit are one. God expresses himself in many forms and many manifestations. If someone wants to argue with you about the bible and if they say that there is no God leave them alone. Just say ok and let them be. As I heard Pastor Walter Hallam of Abundant Life Christian Center says in 1999 while he was teaching repeated what the Apostle Paul said in 1st Corinthians Chapter 14: verse 38: But if any man be ignorant, let him be ignorant. Leave them alone. As I said earlier ignorant is when you don't know. Stupid is when you do know and don't care about the consequences. God, Jesus, and the spirit of the Lord are one and they express themselves the same way. The Holy Spirit is the Holy Ghost they are angels. Now the spirit of the Lord is Gods spirit himself. The Holy Spirit which is the Holy Ghost are angels that are offspring of the spirit of the Lord. The spirit of the Lord is God in animated form. Alive, quickened, and is the manifestation of creation life.

In this Chapter of expressions of God these are just samples of expressions. In other chapters and books we will go deeper into the subject matter. I use this as my motto. For where so ever you're going that's who you're connected too. And whosoever you're connected too that's where you're going.

Chapter 3

The Similitude: of Dreams

L et us go into our subject of dreams. Dreams are
similar in comparison. They are hard to utter at
times as, well as, visions. That's why it is very important
to have a prophet to interpret your dreams if you can't.
The prophet can tell you exactly what God is showing
you. They can reveal to you the secrets that God has
in store for you. For example in the book of Numbers
Chapter 12: verse 8: God tells Aaron, Miriam, and
Moses that the similitude of the Lord shall a prophet
behold. In verse 6: God says that he will speak to his
servant the prophet in a dream. The 1st level into the
dealings of dreams is to know that when God shows
you dreams know at that time that he is trying to
communicate with you.

Key Point # 11:
Your anointing comes by doing something opposite
of your gift. Luke Chapter 16: 10-12: God tests you
by having you serve to keep you humble for his will.
God test you in a few things in places of discomfort.

If found faithful over the few things he will entrust unto you your own stuff. These are the secret laws of manifestations.

Matthew 24: 45-47: The bible says in the book of John Chapter 14: verse 2: In my Father's house are many mansions: if it were not so, I would have told you. I go to prepare a place for you. The word houses means when God changes our corruptible body and gives us a glorious angelic body. It also means levels, realms, and dimensions. Just like there are stairs and each step represents a level, corridor, or passageway we as human beings have different components and departments. For example my big brother Bishop A. did a teaching in Crosby Texas in 2007 called Finding your call and working your assignment; and he talked about once you have your life straight then you can walk into your calling. The teaching that he taught deals with the anatomy of the body by getting control over yourself. Your physical body is like a car and you must speak over your life in order to get control over it or it will run you. Bishop A. is writing a book called Commander and Chief. Get the book. I know it's going to truly revolutionize your life. These are examples dealing with the arenas which still take us to the subject of our Chapter 4: the similitude of dreams. Similitudes referring to similar that sometimes makes them hard to understand if you are not in tune with the spirit of God. What make dreams so hard to understand are the dark speeches that they have. A lot of people when they have dreams really don't understand them. So what ends up happening is that they forget about their dream. They do not write their dream down because of their lack of understanding. The bible says that in the book of Hosea Chapter 4: verse 6: My people are destroyed for lack of knowledge: because thou hast rejected knowledge, I will also reject thee, that thou shalt be no priest to me: seeing thou hast forgotten the law of thy God, I will also forget thy children. Dreams are a typology of Gods' voice. It's symbolic unto the word of the Lord. God uses dreams the similitude's to speak unto us. People are being destroyed every day in their situations because of their lack of understand of dreams. Those who ignore and reject the word of God he will reject them. God will reject their children. Do you see how vital it is to follow instructions? In the book of Proverbs Chapter 4: verse 7: Wisdom is the principal thing; therefore get wisdom: and with all thy getting get understanding. People are not taught as God was referring to his preachers in the book of Hosea Chapter 4: verse 6: that his people are destroyed for a lack of knowledge. The priests were doing what they wanted to do and not teaching Gods people the truth. So God said that he would reject them and forget their children because of their acts of disobedience.

Key Point # 12
You're not responsible for what people do to you. God will hold you responsible for what you do to people. (Mt 24:48-51):

Whatever you do will affect generations positively or negatively. 1st Corinthians 8:9-13: The word of God is top priority. God was telling the priest the ministers that it's their fault that his people are being destroyed. God instructed them with the responsibility to teach his people the word of God. And the priest didn't do as the Lord wanted and the same thing is happening today. Not every preacher is false. Remember there is good and bad in every profession. Even if a minister is doing wrong you just pray for them that God will deal with their hearts to repent. It is not our job to judge. We judge by the spirit of discernment. For when we judge verbally we at that same time bring damnation unto ourselves. Matthew Chapter 7: verses 1-5: Judge not, that ye be not judged. 2 For with what judgment ye judge, ye shall be judged: and with what measure ye mete, it shall be measured to you again. 3 And why beholdest thou the mote that is in thy brother's eye, but considerest not the beam that is in thine own eye? 4.Or how wilt thou say to thy brother, let me pull out the mote out of thine eye; and, behold, a beam is in thine own eye? 5.Thou hypocrite, first cast out the beam out of thine own eye; and then shalt thou see clearly to cast out the mote out of thy brother's eye. In the book of Proverbs Chapter 4: verse 7: it states that wisdom is the principal thing which is the highest established law of God. It is Gods' word. Gods' principal. Gods' ordinance. Gods' statutes. Gods' commandments. Gods' law. Gods' precepts. God puts his word above him. Wisdom is the voice of God. Wisdom is the application of knowledge.

In order to get wisdom the bible states that in the book of James Chapter 1: verse 5: If any of you lack wisdom, let him ask of God, that giveth to all men liberally, and upbraideth not; and it shall be given him. God will give you the wisdom, knowledge, and the understanding to interpret dreams and visions. It does you no good if you have knowledge and no understanding. Knowledge with wisdom from God gives you an understanding. Wisdom is the application of knowledge. If you do not practice writing down your dreams and visions you will forget them.

Key Point # 13
Writing down your dreams and visions summons angels to work on your behalf. Angels love writing. This is known as the law of writing. Angels hearken unto the voice of Gods' word. Psalms 103:20:

What we think about becomes thoughts or the meditation of an ideal. Thoughts become ideals into imagination acted upon by faith produces manifestation. The bible says that in the book of Joshua Chapter 1: verse 8: This book of the law shall not depart out of thy mouth; but thou shalt meditate therein day and night, that thou mayest observe to do according to all that is written therein: for then thou shalt make thy way prosperous, and then thou shalt have good success. By meditating and thinking about something it will grow. We become whatsoever we allow into our hearts. I heard Bishop A. tell me a few years ago that whatsoever you set your mind to attract will become attracted to you. This is a universal principal. I always say if you want to know where a person is at in life listen to them speak for the first few seconds to the first few minutes and they will a lot of time tell you where they are at in life. The bible says that in the book of Luke Chapter 6: verse 45: which basically says that whatever a person talks about a whole lot is their abundance. It's their treasure that is stored in their hearts. I use to have a lot of dreams for many years. Now the Lord only shows and reveals to me visions. I have been writing down my dreams since November of 1999. I meditate upon the word of God everyday all the time because I do meditate upon the word of God every day, I am able to interpret dreams and visions. The spirit of God reveals unto me what they mean. The bible says that in the book of Proverbs Chapter 1: verse 6: To understand a proverb, and the interpretation; the words of the wise, and their dark sayings. A proverb is the words of the wise. Proverbs are dark sayings illustrations of the kingdom of God kingdom of heaven. The kingdom of God is the power. The kingdom of heaven is a place. God uses parables which proverbs are a little more advanced that parable to get people to understand what he is saying. The Lord uses parables to get people to understand the kingdom. Remember that our economics comes from God. For examples Jesus told Nicodemus that in the book of John Chapter 3: that if he can't understand earthly things how he can understand heavenly things. And that's why God uses parables because a lot of people do not understand the things of the spirit. I'm talking about people in the church. People who been in church for decades. I have seen this and have witnessed this with my own eyes time after time. Many people do not understand the knowledge of the Kingdom. So the Lord when referring unto the Kingdom uses parables and proverbs to tell them about the kingdom on an earthly level so that they may understand what he is saying. Parables and proverbs are dreams and visions expressed verbally in a realm that many do not know how to tap into. They do not understand the dark sayings. The dark sayings of old are now being revealed through Jesus Christ. Jesus said that in the book of Matthew Chapter 5: verse 8: blessed are the pure in heart, for they shall see God. Which is a proverb, an established principal of God? And you have to envision, imagine yourself picturing, and visualizing things that the Lord is saying unto you. You must have an inclined ear to listen unto what the spirit of God is saying. We as people envision words because they are so powerful unto us. An example is found in the book of Genesis Chapter 1: and God said and it was so. He spoke whatsoever he wanted into existence and called it good. In the book of John Chapter 1: verse 1: In the beginning was the word, and the word was with God, and the word was God. The word is Jesus who is God in the beginning. The word which is God produced and manifested everything that we see. Things we see and don't see. Someone may be ministering the word of God to someone. They may be speaking to them in parables and proverbs which is known as the milk of the word. This Chapter on the similitude of dreams must be seriously addressed to the body of Christ. It must be addressed unto the lost also. Many people have dreams from God but do not understand the seriousness of them. Therefore they are destroyed for the lack of knowledge. In Chapter 5: we are going to talk about a mentoring life coach. One who can nurture your character, gifts, and talents for the purpose of God.

Cherubims: and Seraphims: Volume 2:

Cherubims: and Seraphims are celestial angels. They are beautiful heavenly creatures. They are living creatures. Ezekiel Chapter 1: Hebrews 13:2: And be not forgetful to entertain strangers; for thereby some have entertained angels unawares. There are angels all around us and with us. There are angels who govern the waters known, as Mermaids. Revelations Chapter 5:13. And every creature; which is in heaven, and on the earth, and such as are in the sea, and all that are in them, heard : saying, blessing, and honor, and glory, and power, be unto him that sitteth upon the throne, and unto the lamb forever and ever. There are angels in heaven where God is. There are angels in the 2nd heaven known, as outer-space; the sphere, or dimension that is outward beyond the bio-spheric matrix of the earth. There are angels here on earth under the firmament and in the 3rd heaven. Angels can take shape, and form of people; only for a limited time. They have a mind of their own.

They have a choice as mankind; human-beings to serve God, or not to serve God. Exodus 23:20: these angels are assigned to assist Gods people in their life. They are the angelic hosts. They are the living-creatures. They are here to prepare the way. Beware of these angels voices because whosoever blasphemes against these angels (Holy Ghost): go against God. Matthew 12:31: Wherefore I say unto you, All manner of sin and blasphemy shall be forgiven unto men: but the blasphemy against the Holy Ghost, shall not be forgiven unto men. These angels come to drive the demons the demoniacs; unclean spirits: Dt 7:1-6; out of the lands, and countries. Serve no other God but God. Serve not the nations God. For God is a jealous God: Ex 20:3-5: Gods angels will bless our bread, and water: by manifesting favor; Isaiah 43:3: and God will give us the treasure; of: darkness, and hidden riches of: secret places they are hidden and our angels will reveal them unto us. verse 25. God promises to take away sickness away from us. He promises in verse 26. That he will extend long life unto us. Verse 27: God will send his fear, which are his angels to cause our enemies to turn their backs unto us. Demons are angels also and these angels will cause our enemies to turn their backs unto us. Angels are very stubborn especially Cherubims and Seraphims. They will only do what Gods people say, but with a right motive according to the will of God. These angels have the super natural uncanny ability to take possession of peoples bodies. They are with us at all times. Genesis 3:24: So he drove out the man; and he placed at the east of the garden of Eden Cherubims, and a flaming sword which turned every way of the tree of life. Angels are here and they are assigned to keep us in all our ways, and if we go against the word of God which is Gods instructions they will turn on, and against you.

Chapter 4

Life Coaches

The bible says that in the book of Isaiah Chapter 49: verse 23: and kings shall be thy nursing fathers, and their queens thy nursing mothers: they shall bow down to thee with their face toward the earth, and lick up the dust of thy feet; and thou shalt know that I am the Lord: for they shall not be ashamed that wait for me. A spiritual father or spiritual mother is someone who will invest time into your life for the purpose of God for your destiny. One of the main reasons why the people especially youths are out of control is because their parents are not stepping up to do what God has ordained for them to do. In the book of Proverbs Chapter 22: verse 6: Train up a child in the way he should go and when he is old, he will not depart from it. So beyond a shadow of a doubt training must be displayed in peoples' lives. Even adults must walk in maturity. Just because a person is considered an adult does not mean that they are mature in the things of God. I see the generations even this generation in 2014 wants to be grown before their time and that's where a coach comes in to help nurture, develop their gifts and talents in them. Every young person wants a role model. Even adults want role models someone to look up too. Parents have been given a mandate from God to train and to teach their children to know about God. And because of the lack of God fearing people our society is totally out of control. That's why the bible says that a child left alone bringeth forth shame, therefore we can go further into training with our kids. This small section can be identified as the root to where coaching can start. Lets' make one thing clear if the parents won't step up to train and to teach their children God will make a way for them. My life has been very hard even as a Christian. There are still trials, tests, and tribulations that we must go through in this life journey, but I'm not alone because God is with me always. I felt like the prophet Isaiah in the book of Isaiah Chapter 49: verses 1-7: 1.Listen, o isles, unto me; and hearken, ye people, from far; the Lord hath called me from the womb; from the bowels of my mother hath he made mention of my name. 2And have made my mouth like a sharp sword; in the shadow of his hand hath he hid me, and made me a polished shaft; in his quiver hath he hid me; 3And said unto me, thou art my servant, o Israel, in whom I will be glorified. 4Then I said, I have labored in vain, I have spent my strength for nought, and in vain: yet surely my judgment is with the Lord, and my work with my God. 5.And now, saith the Lord that formed me from the womb to be his servant, to bring Jacob again to him, though Israel be not gathered, yet shall I be glorious in the eyes of the Lord, and my God shall be my strength. 6 and he said, it is a light thing that thou shouldest be my servant to raise up the tribes of Jacob, and to restore the preserved of Israel: I will also give thee for a light to the gentiles, that thou mayest be my salvation unto the end of the earth. 7 Thus saith the Lord, the redeemer of Israel, and his holy one, to him whom man despiseth, to him whom the nation abhorreth, to a servant of rulers, kings shall see and arise, princes also shall worship, because of the Lord that is faithful, and the holy one of Israel, and he shall choose thee. The bible says that God is a jealous God and that we should have no other Gods before him. God will allow people to despise and to reject you to cause you to stand on your own. When people despise and reject you allow these persecutions to draw you closer to God so that your faith and dependency will not be in man, but in God. Despite the situation and circumstances if God be for us who can be against us? I have experienced these things ever since I was a child and I did not understand why people hated me so much. Now lets' look at the rest of the verse. The bible says that in the book of Isaiah Chapter 49: verse 7: Thus saith the Lord, the Redeemer of Israel, and his holy one, to him whom man despiseth, to him whom the nation abhorreth, to a servant of rulers, Kings shall see and arise, princes also shall worship, because of the Lord that is faithful, and the Holy One of Israel, and he shall choose thee. Now we can see and conclude that God promotes his servants by causing the nations of the world to see his glory on his people which leads me to say verse 7: of Isaiah Chapter 49: is like a training camp for his people. There really is no real life coach but Jesus Christ the son of God. When you are under someone's' mentorship they are responsible for your training. My ministry is a prophetic outreach ministry and the Lord has taught me about my ministry on many occasions. In the book of John Chapter 10: verse 27: My sheep hear my voice, and I know them, and they follow me: A coach can be referred to as a mentor or a counselor. One who pushes you into your purpose and warns you about pitfalls to avoid. They give you instruction and guidance. You should do better than your mentor because not only are you going to have your own personal experiences, but your mentor is pouring their life into you for your divine purpose. A life coach is someone who has a lot of experience in the area in which they teach. It's like a pastor who leads Gods people into their God given purpose. One thing that brought me to tears in the summer of 2001 was when the Lord told me to turn to the book of Isaiah Chapter 42: verses 1-4: which talks about his people going through things to mature them in who he has predestined them to be. And by them going through things they will metamorphs into Israel which is a prince over his people. God promised that he would be with us no matter what and that these trials would not kill us. The benefits are great because he promised to give men in exchange for our lives. One thing that Jesus said that would always be with us is in the book of John

Chapter 16: verse 33: These things I have spoken unto you, that in me ye might have peace. In the world ye shall have tribulation: but be of good cheer; I have overcome the world. He says that as long as we are here on this earth and in this flesh that we are going to experience trouble. God gives us his peace even though we are having trouble. We have his word that comforts us no matter what is going on. All hell can break loose all around us but it will not bother us. He said be of good cheer which is his word because he has overcome the world. Our greatest example to follow after is Jesus Christ the son of the living God. He is a life coach unto us all. In the book of Matthew Chapter 28: verse 20: Teaching them to observe all things whatsoever I have commanded you: and, lo, I am with you alway, even unto the end of the world. Amen. So Jesus is always with us. Jesus Christ is our prime example to follow. Dreams and visions are coaches because they show and reveal unto us things that are about to come. John Chapter 16: verse 13: Howbeit when he, the Spirit of truth, is come, he will guide you into all truth: for he shall not speak of himself; but whatsoever he shall hear, that shall he speak: and he will show you things to come. Jesus states that the Holy Ghost is the comforter which is a life coach. The Holy Ghost is the Holy Spirit for they are angels. They are just like Jesus. They come not to do their own will but God's will. A pastor is a life coach. Jeremiah 3: 15: And I will give you pastors according to mine heart, which shall feed you with knowledge and understanding. A life coach is one who will mentor you in the ways of God. A school coach can be a life coach. A lot of coaches are life coaches whether they realize it or not. Many teachers are life coaches also. Teachers, counselors, coaches, instructors are just like parents unto a lot of people. So many young people are going astray in the wrong direction. The bible says that in the book of Proverbs that a child left alone bringeth forth shame. Mentors are great coaches that try to motivate people to move into their destiny. Let's look at Jesus our great example. He mentored a lot of people especially the 12 disciples. Even though Judas Iscariot betrayed him Jesus still loved him.

Key Point # 14:
Not everyone who you invest your time in will follow your guidance and direction. Everyone is given a choice. Those who turn on you, betray you, reject you, lie on you, and even try and kill you are in actuality preparing you for your next level of elevation.

Even my position as an Apostle causes me to be a mentor unto others. God coaches and instructs us continually. God spoke unto Solomon and told him that he would bless him because of his father David. God told Solomon that he would make his kingdom last forever and that he would always keep him on the throne if he would keep his ordinances. But in the book of 1st Kings Chapter 11: verses 1-11: But King Solomon loved many strange women, together with the daughter of pharaoh, women of the Moabites,

Ammonites, Edomites, Zidonians, and Hittites11:2: Of the nations concerning which the Lord said unto the children of Israel, ye shall not go in to them, neither shall they come in unto you: for surely they will turn away your heart after their Gods: Solomon clave unto these in love. 11:3 And he had seven hundred wives, princesses, and three hundred concubines: and his wives turned away his heart. 11:4 For it came to pass, when Solomon was old, that his wives turned away his heart after other Gods: and his heart was not perfect with the Lord his God, as was the heart of David his father. 11:5 For Solomon went after Ashtoreth the Goddess of the Zidonians, and after Milcom the abomination of the ammonites. 11:6 And Solomon did evil in the sight of the Lord, and went not fully after the Lord, as did David his father. 11:7 Then did Solomon build a high place for Chemosh, the abomination of Moab, in the hill that is before Jerusalem, and for Molech, the abomination of the children of Ammon. 11:8 And likewise did he for all his strange wives, which burnt incense and sacrificed unto their Gods. 11:9 And the Lord was angry with Solomon, because his heart was turned from the Lord God of Israel, which had appeared unto him twice, 11:10 And had commanded him concerning this thing, that he should not go after other Gods: but he kept not that which the Lord commanded.11:11 Wherefore the Lord said unto Solomon, forasmuch as this is done of thee, and thou hast not kept my covenant and my statutes, which I have commanded thee, I will surely rend the kingdom from thee, and will give it to thy servant. We see that King Solomon loved many strange women who served other Gods. They turned his heart away from the Lord. Solomon had let the Gods of these strange women turn him away from God. He let the other Gods be his god and coach him to serve idols and things sacrificed unto devils. So it is our choice who we allow to coach us. There are great benefits in letting someone invest into your life. The bible says that in the book of John Chapter 14: verse 12: Verily, verily, I say unto you, He that believeth on me, the works that I do shall he do also; and greater works than these shall he do; because I go unto my Father. Because the disciples allowed Jesus to mentor them the majority of them became very successful. So by us following someone who knows God the benefits that we get is that persons mantel. The word mantel means simply defined, are spiritual garments of authority that endow the wearer with supernatural grace to establish the kingdom of heaven in the earthly realm. Mantel-represents spiritual covering usually refer to spiritual authority and anointing. As an apostle I mentor people with the gifts and talents that God has given me. The question is are you willing to mentor people because you were placed here on this earth for a special purpose to help others. Jesus says that no greater love is this than that a man lay down his life for his friends. This simply means to put others first instead of yourself. Dreams and visions can mentor you only with the proper understanding of what they mean. They must line up with the bible which is the word of God. I like wrestling and I think a lot of times that they are like mentors to me. Such as Sting, Ric Flair, Hulk Hogan, Bret Hart, the Macho Man and many more. I have always been a very great fan of wrestling. I enjoy wrestling and practicing wrestling moves. One thing that the Lord told us in the book of Jeremiah Chapter 33: verse 3: Call unto me, and I will answer thee, and shew thee great and mighty things, which thou knowest not. This is a promise from the Lord that if we would pray he will reveal unto us things that we do not know and there are many examples of life coaches in the bible. There are also many life coaches today in the world that we live in.

Chapter 5

Self Analysis: Character Identification Code

W ho are you is a common question that is asked about people and the greatest example that we have is Jesus Christ because he knew who he was. He knows who he is even now for he forever lieveth. One statement that he made in the book of John Chapter 3: verse 16: For God so loved the world, that he gave his only begotten son, that whosoever believeth in him should not perish, but have everlasting life. He was saying as a messenger of God that God his father gave him as a sacrificial lamb to die for the sins of humanity. If anyone believes in Jesus would not go to hell but will have heaven as their home. There are many examples of Jesus when referring to who he was, but we see the transformations in the book of Revelation Chapter 1: verses 10-20: I was in the spirit on the Lord's day, and heard behind me a great voice, as of a trumpet, 11 saying, I am alpha and omega, the first and the last: and, what thou seest, write in a book, and send it unto the seven churches which are in Asia; unto Ephesus, and unto Smyrna, and unto bergamots, and unto Thyatira, and unto Sardis, and unto Philadelphia, and unto Laodicea. 12 And I turned to see the voice that spake with me. And being turned, I saw seven golden candlesticks; 13 And in the midst of the seven candlesticks one like unto the Son of man, clothed with a garment down to the foot, and girt about the paps with a golden girdle. 14 His head and his hairs were white like wool, as white as snow; and his eyes were as a flame of fire; 15 And his feet like unto fine brass, as if they burned in a furnace; and his voice as the sound of many waters. 16 And he had in his right hand seven stars: and out of his mouth went a sharp two-edged sword: and his countenance was as the sun shineth in his strength. 17 And when I saw him, I fell at his feet as dead. And he laid his right hand upon me, saying unto me, fear not; I am the first and the last: 18 I am he that liveth, and was dead; and, behold, I am alive for evermore, amen; and have the keys of hell and of death. 19 Write the things which thou hast seen, and the things which are, and the things which shall be hereafter; 20 The mystery of the seven stars which thou sawest in my right hand, and the seven golden candlesticks. The seven stars are the angels of the seven churches: and the seven candlesticks which thou sawest are the seven churches. A total transformation transformed Jesus to the point that John said that Jesus was liken unto the son of man because of the glory of God that was in his life. He had a garment down to his foot and girt about the paps with a golden girdle.

The robe represented purification, sanctification, and righteousness. It also represents the book of Leviticus which means priesthood, holiness, and access unto God. Jesus represented a true and only eternal sacrificial priest of God. Not only that Jesus is our high priest the one who sanctifies us from our sins. The bible says that Jesus hair was white like wool, as white as snow which represents purification and sanctification. His eyes were as the flame of fire which represents that God is a consuming fire that comes to try the hearts of men. So he is the son because the bible says that the eyes are the windows to the soul. That fire consumes everything that it touches. When he looks at someone or something he consumes them by trying their hearts. His feet were like fine brass, as if they burned in a furnace. This is another implication that his steps are ordered and directed always. His voice sounded like the voice of many waters. Revelation Chapter 1: verse 15: And his feet like unto fine brass, as if they burned in a furnace; and his voice as the sound of many waters. John Chapter 7: verse 38: He that believeth on me, as the scripture hath said, out of his belly shall flow rivers of living water. The rivers of living waters are the answers to life. There are streams of spiritual waters waiting for us as believers in Christ Jesus. The bible says that he had in his right hand seven stars which is the spirit of the Lord. Jesus said that all power is given unto him in heaven and in earth. Matthew 28:18: And Jesus came and spake unto them, saying, all power is given unto me in heaven and in earth. God has given us power over the devil and his forces. The right hand represents authority and the left hand represents judgment. The scripture said that out of his mouth went a sharp two-edged sword which is the word of God. It says also in the book of Hebrews Chapter 4: verses 12- 13: 12. For the word of God is quick, and powerful, and sharper than any two-edged sword, piercing even to the dividing asunder of soul and spirit, and of the joints and marrow, and is a discerner of the thoughts and intents of the heart. 13. Neither is there any creature that is not manifest in his sight: but all things are naked and opened unto the eyes of him with whom we have to do. The scripture is saying that Jesus countenance was as the sun shineth in his strength. This is everlasting joy. For the joy of the Lord is our strength. This is saying that joy was all on Jesus face just like it was in the old testament when Moses came down from off of the mountain. The glory of God was so strong on him that the people could not look at his face. They could not look at his face because the fulfillment of the law had not come. The children of Israel could not understand what was being said due to the spiritual veil that had covered their eyes. As the scripture says that the law was our school master to guide us until Christ came on the scene, which is the fulfillment of the law so that our eyes could be opened to see the things of God that has been hidden for ages. In verse 17: John said that he saw him and fell down at his feet as dead and Jesus laid his right hand upon him saying fear not I am the 1st and the last. He was in the presence of God. He saw the radiance of God that instantly knocked and forced him unto his feet in shock. He manifested himself unto the Apostle John as God almighty. The reason why Jesus kept saying that he was the son of God was because the people could not receive him as God. When Jesus said that he was the son of God unto the Scribes and Pharisees they started to stone him. So guess what if they could not receive God as the son they wouldn't receive him as the father. You can just imagine that in the mind of the Apostle John that he could not comprehend the totality that Jesus was and is God.

Key Point # 14:
When you come to the truth that Jesus is God a lot of people will leave you because that's where they are at. They won't understand. People don't have a problem with what you do. People have a problem of who you become.

Moses saw the back of God and he saw Gods glory. The Apostle John saw God as who he really was manifested in glory; which caused the Apostle John to begin to write the book of Revelation as he was instructed of by the Lord. John saw apocalyptic visions in which many theologians write that the book of Revelation is the war of Christ verses the devil. Christ wins and the devil loses. What was running through the Apostle Johns mind when Jesus told him to fear not; I am the first and the last was a total shock unto him? To me personally that would bring me to tears. As the scripture said that in the book of Revelation Chapter 7: verses 15-17: 15. Therefore are they before the throne of God, and serve him day and night in his temple: and he that sitteth on the throne shall dwell among them. 16. They shall hunger no more, neither thirst anymore; neither shall the sun light on them, nor any heat. 17. For the lamb which is in the midst of the throne shall feed them, and shall lead them unto living fountains of waters: and God shall wipe away all tears from their eyes. Jesus told John to fear not. To hear those words that Jesus said to the Apostle John is on a high level that broke the spirit of fear from John. For example in the book of Isaiah Chapter 41: verses 10-12: 10. Fear thou not; for I am with thee: be not dismayed; for I am thy God: I will strengthen thee; yea, I will help thee; yea, I will uphold thee with the right hand of my righteousness. 11. They that were incensed against thee shall be ashamed and confounded: they shall be as nothing; and they that strive with thee shall perish. 12. Thou shalt seek them, and shalt not find them, even them that contended with thee: they that war against thee shall be as nothing, and as a thing of nought. These words in the book of Revelation Chapter 1: verse 17: is saying fear not I am the first and the last are words that signify that there are no more enemies, because every knee shall bow and every tongue shall confess that Jesus Christ is Lord. He is saying that he is the father. He Jesus is a holy earthly form come down unto humanity to save that his creation. Christ sits at the right hand of God. Christ is God. If therefore Christ sits at the right hand of God he can be in heaven and on earth whenever he feels like it. God is bound by his own law. Christ sits down on the right hand of God making intercession for the saints of God. He says that in the book of Isaiah Chapter 49: verse 6: Thus saith the Lord the king of Israel, and his redeemer the Lord of hosts; I am the first, and I am the last; and beside me there is no God. Jesus told John that I am he that liveth and was dead, and behold I am alive for evermore amen. And have the keys of hell and of death. He states that not only is he forever and eternally alive he died to the flesh of his body. He laid down his life by putting himself last in order to redeem sinful man back unto him by his ultimate sacrifice. He says and behold I am alive forever more and just as the scripture said that we are changed from glory to glory. In Johns mind for him to see Christ and not recognize him then to see him as the Christ is a statement that causes the natural mind to know and realize that nothing can stop Jesus, nor stop you. When you come into the presence of God you will never be the same again. For greater is Christ in us than he that is in the world. Jesus is the eternal life force himself. He is the life source himself. He says that he has the keys of hell and of death meaning that as he said in the book of Matthew Chapter 28: verse 18: And Jesus came and spake unto them, saying, all power is given unto me in heaven and in earth. Christ has the authority to open and close any door in any person's life. Now this is someone with all power that would most definitely convince me to trust in him. He told John to write the things down which he had seen and the things which are and the things which shall be hereafter which is prophecy. As the scripture says that the testimony of Jesus is the spirit of prophecy. Jesus then tells John about the mystery of the seven stars and seven golden candlesticks. Johns mind was beyond a shadow of a doubt on a higher level than ever before that accelerated his spirit. We as a people, the body of Christ must buy a mind. We must marry a mind. I heard the Master prophet Bishop E Bernard Jordan say that. As the scripture saith so as a man thinketh in his heart so is he. Everything that is in the world is already in you. We have to know how to draw it out and know how to use what God gave us properly. Even God has thoughts which means that he has a mind. God has a brain. In the book of Jeremiah Chapter 29: verse 11: For I know the thoughts that I think toward you, saith the Lord, thoughts of peace, and not of evil, to give you an expected end. So God has a mind and he expresses his emotions. But God doesn't change as stated in the book of Malachi Chapter 3: verse 6: For I am the Lord, I change not; therefore ye sons of Jacob are not consumed. I heard Bishop Jordan say that as I stated earlier that you must buy a mind by getting knowledge of the word of God; to use the knowledge that God has given you with wisdom to prosper for Gods purpose. Our minds are just like Gods mind but we are limited if we lean unto our own understanding. We have the Holy Spirit which is the comforter as Jesus stated in the book of John Chapter 16: verse 13: Howbeit when he, the spirit of truth, is come, he will guide you into all truth: for he shall not speak of himself; but whatsoever he shall hear, that shall he speak: and he will shew you things to come. In the book of 1st Corinthians Chapter 2: verse 16: For who hath known the mind of the Lord, that he may instruct him? But we have the mind of Christ. This text indicates that we have no excuses about knowing God. Gods' word is will which is his word. In the book of James Chapter 1: verse 5: If any of you lack wisdom, let him ask of God, that giveth to all men liberally, and upbraideth not; and it shall be given him. So even though we are limited as human beings we have God living in us. Even as Jesus stated in John Chapter 7: verses 37-38: 37. In the last day, that great day of the feast, Jesus stood and cried, saying, if any man thirst, let him come unto me, and drink. 38. He that believeth on me, as the scripture hath said, out of his belly shall flow rivers of living water. The scripture is referring to the Holy Ghost being inside of us, and not only do we have waters but we have living waters which is all the answers to life. Streams of the word of God, streams of rivers of living waters are within us as believers. There are portals and doors that God has for us. We as born again believers have the mind of Christ. God gives us wisdom and if we desire it we just ask God to let the living waters of life flow through us to download through our minds. The Holy Spirit will tell us by revealing unto us what God is saying. Whatever you pay mind to you purchase. You can give that product away. Mind has the money back guarantee. So don't complain when you purchase that thought. You can return that thought back where you got it from. As God said in the Old Testament that he have set before us life or death. He tells us to choose life that we and our seed may live. Isn't that a good shepherd to guide us through life? Christ is the door all that ever came before him were thieves and robbers. The thieves and robbers were and are false-religions. They are cults set up by the devil pretending to be of God. These are devils working signs, and lying wonders that are setup to deceive even the very elect. Christ is God and Christ is the only way to the father. Even though Christ is the father he can do whatsoever he wants. For God so loved the world that he gave his only begotten son that whosoever believeth in him should not perish but have everlasting life. That everlasting life is a guarantee that you as a saved born again believer will not go to the lake of fire. Hell is opposite of paradise. Hell is a spiritual prison in which the soul of the sinner who would not repent is. Hell is a guarantee ticket unto the lake of fire. Paradise is a realm and dimension that is a guaranteed ticket unto heaven.

Key Point: # 15:
The anointing that was in the seventies, eighties, nineties, and in 2000 is old wine; old anointing. What God is doing now in 2013 unto 2020 is a 7 year period in which we the church shall begin to see God flood his people with great power than ever before. The devil has been allowed to upgrade his game. The devil

is still coming at Gods people the same way, but the strategy of the devil has mightily increased because of sin. Sin is magnifying at rapid, quantum rates but the bible says that if sin abounds then the grace of God shall abound more. A lot of pastors on t.v. God is pulling down but not all of them. The majority of them are hirelings. We are about to see jezebels workers falling down dead slain. These are hirelings, false prophets, wolves in sheep's' clothing. These do not care about Gods people but are only after filthy lucre. They only want money.

I hear the word of the Lord saying that many false prophets are rising not just in the church but in every aspect of secular-society. Many are coming and shall come with a form of Godliness but denying the power of our Lord Jesus Christ. Many in the church shall fall away by the multitudes but at the same time God is not only bringing people into the churches. God is causing even celebrities, famous people, rich, and wealthy people to get saved, delivered, and healed. God is turning these leaders into instruments for his purpose. Agape love is the love of God. It's neither fake nor imitation. It's Gods nature, character, divinity, and essence. I have seen so many pastors in the churches pretending to walk in God's love then turn on you. They turn because they found out that God was about to elevate and raise you up and they got jealous. Beware of the leaven of the scribes and Pharisees which is hypocrisy.

Key Point # 16:
God will allow you to be amongst the religious secta the scribes, Pharisees, and Sadducees for them to give you their wealth; which is the knowledge, and understanding of the things of God. God allows you to be rejected and casted out from amongst them because when you come to a level of maturity to stand on your own it's time to move on.

They can only give you knowledge, and understanding of the things of God but wisdom comes from God himself. Remember that when you are rejected and casted out of the church then this is a sign of elevation and promotion from God. We must ask God to give us the presence of mind of the season that we are in. We must ask God to reveal and show unto us the season that we are about to walk into and the seasons to come. Jesus said that in the book of John Chapter 10: verse 11: I am the good shepherd: the good shepherd giveth his life for the sheep. Such a great example as I mentioned earlier that Jesus Christ the son of the living God is our greatest example to follow. Leaders make great leaders. Dreams and visions are revealed to the mind of that which the Holy Spirit reveals to our spirit that is visually pictured unto the mind.

Key Point # 17:
We have many minds that we must awaken. We have minds that are at a very high mastery level. We have minds that are asleep. We must awaken those minds by

tapping unto our fullest potential. God has placed the secrets inside of every born again believer but it takes the Holy Ghost to reveal them unto us. Remember that we have this treasure in earthen vessel inside of us. For in Gods mansion there are many mansions which means that this corruptible shall take on immortality. Let's go to the book of 1st Corinthians Chapter 2: verses 14-16: 14.But the natural man receiveth not the things of the spirit of God: for they are foolishness unto him: neither can he know them, because they are spiritually discerned. 15. But he that is spiritual judgeth all things, yet he himself is judged of no man. 16. For who hath known the mind of the Lord, that he may instruct him? But we have the mind of Christ. For even as an unsaved person cannot understand and comprehend the word of God. So it is to the saved person that has confessed Jesus Christ as their personal Lord and savior that they can understand the mysteries of God. When we have dreams and visions at night time or during different times through the day we do not understand what God has showed us until we seek him by prayer. He said that if we lacked wisdom he will give it unto us. James Chapter 1: verse 5: If any of you lack wisdom, let him ask of God, that giveth to all men liberally, and upbraideth not; and it shall be given him. The bible says that the things of God are foolishness unto the non-believer because the spirit that an unsaved person has is dead and not alive unto Christ. The flesh is only accustomed unto what it sees, hears, touches, taste, and smells in the world. This is known as the 5 senses or the sensory-mechanism. The sensory-mechanism is the physical-body. Therefore the apostle Paul said that I give you milk and not meat because the people were not ready to receive the word of God. They did not understand the mysteries of the kingdom. Even as Christians we have to go through trials, tests, and tribulations to crucify the flesh to make us stronger in Christ. These tribulations mature us to let us know who we are in Christ so that we can be and walk as over comers in life. The flesh wants to be God and he said that we shall have no other God before him. Exodus Chapter 20: verse 3: Thou shalt have no other Gods before me. Neither can the carnal fleshly man know the mysteries of God because they are spiritually discerned from him. The bible says that in the book of Proverbs Chapter 4: verse 7: Wisdom is the principal thing; therefore get wisdom: and with all thy getting get understanding. The natural man cannot understand the kingdom of God. Nor can he understand the kingdom of heaven. Gods' word is the highest thing there is. God has placed his word over him and God stands by his word to perform his word. Isaiah 58: verses 8-11: 8.For my thoughts are not your thoughts, neither are your ways my ways, saith the Lord. 9. For as the heavens are higher than the earth, so are my ways higher than your ways, and my thoughts than your thoughts. 10. For as the rain cometh down, and the snow from heaven, and returneth not thither, but watereth the earth, and maketh it bring forth and bud, that it may give seed to the sower, and bread to the eater: 11. So shall my word be that goeth forth out of my mouth: it shall not return unto me void, but it shall accomplish that which I please, and it shall prosper in the thing whereto I sent it. The bible says that in the book of 1st Corinthians 2: 15: But he that is spiritual judgeth all things, yet he himself is judged of no man. The scripture is saying that those who are saved by confessing Jesus Christ as their personal Lord and Savior are not condemned to the devils system. And what is the devils system? The devils system is to kill, steal, and to destroy. John Chapter 10: verse 10: The thief cometh not, but for to steal, and to kill, and to destroy: I am come that they might have life, and that they might have it more abundantly. 2nd Corinthians Chapter 2: verse 11: Lest satan should get an advantage of us: for we are not ignorant of his devices. The devils devices are his onslaughts, tactics, schemes, whiles, and weaponry. Matthew Chapter 24: verses 4-5: 4. And Jesus answered and said unto them, take heed that no man deceive you. 5. For many shall come in my name, saying, I am Christ; and shall deceive many. Jesus told his disciples to take heed that no man deceive them. The reason why he told them to take heed was because of the deception of satan. This is one of satans deceptions in verse 5. Christ said for many shall come in my name saying that they are the Christ and shall deceive many. These are people in the church and in the world, people pretending to come from God and to be of God but they are false prophet's wolves in sheep's clothing. Having a form of Godliness but the denying the power of God. They shall be under demonic influence pretending to be good. They shall try and ask you a lot of questions in order to find out what you know so that they may use your information against you. Another deception of satan is in the book of John Chapter 16: verses 1-4: 1. These things have I spoken unto you, that ye should not be offended. 2. They shall put you out of the synagogues: yea, the time cometh, that whosoever killeth you will think that he doeth God service. 3. And these things will they do unto you, because they have not known the father, nor me. 4. But these things have I told you, that when the time shall come, ye may remember that I told you of them. And these things I said not unto you at the beginning, because I was with you. A deception of the devil is to get you offended so by this weapon it will throw you off track. Satan's job is to steal, kill, and to destroy you by making you offended and the scripture said do not grieve the Holy Spirit. Ephesians Chapter 4: verse 30: And grieve not the Holy Spirit of God, whereby ye are sealed unto the day of redemption. This is how the devil comes in like a flood when you are offended. At that time demons are allowed to invade your life by the multitudes because of unforgiveness. Jesus states in verse 2: that they shall put you out of the synagogues which are the churches. That they shall kick you out of the churches because they are offended of who you are in Christ. Back then when Christ was on in the earth over 2000 years ago and when he was going to leave he said that whosoever killeth thee will think that they are doing what God wants them to do. This is demonic deception. People become offended at you because of who you are in Christ and they think by lying on you, stealing from you, using you by trying to literally kill you that they are doing what God wants them to do. There are people especially in the churches who will try and literally kill you because they think God is leading them to do this. They will try and kill you because it makes them feel real good about themselves. They will do all these things unto you because they do not know God, nor Christ. Christ said and these things I said not unto you at the beginning because I was with you which means that we have multitudes of angels with us. Our angels hearken unto the voice of Gods' word. As we pray angels are dispatched. So the devil and his army of demons know that your hedge of protection is low. They will try and invade us by coming against our mind. The helmet of salvation protects our mind from condemnation. That's why we must be prayed up, fasting having on the breastplate of righteousness, having our loins girded up with truth, and having our feet shod with the preparation of the gospel of peace. We as believers in Christ must have on the shield of faith at all times. Above all using the sword of the spirit whereby we shall be able to quench all the fiery darts of the wicked one.

Key Point # 18:
The devil shall by demon demonic influence by the spirit of jezebel have many coming to you in the name of the Lord saying they are the Christ, and shall deceive

many, but not you. When the deception and offences try and come at you know at that time and season of your life that the Holy Ghost is about to show and reveal to you things that you have prayed about. John Chapter 16: verses 13- 15: 13. Howbeit when he, the Spirit of truth, is come, he will guide you into all truth: for he shall not speak of himself; but whatsoever he shall hear, that shall he speak: and he will shew you things to come. 14. He shall glorify me: for he shall receive of mine, and shall shew it unto you. 15. All things that the Father hath are mine: therefore said I, that he shall take of mine, and shall shew it unto you.

The psychology is to know when the enemy comes in like a flood that the spirit of God will lift up a standard. At the time of the warfare know that doors have been opened up unto you. For the just shall walk by faith and not by sight. Romans Chapter 8: verse 1: There is therefore now no condemnation to them which are in Christ Jesus, who walk not after the flesh, but after the spirit. Condemnation is a weapon, tool, and device of the devil. The devil can longer control us as born again Holy Ghost filled believers. Now the devil can demonically oppress us by demons and unclean spirits. Once you are saved, baptized, and filled with the Holy Spirit you can no longer be possessed. The devil can no longer control us as born again believers in the Lord Jesus Christ. Because of the fall of man in the garden mankind was under judgment, but Christ Jesus has come to set us free from condemnation. Jesus stated that and you shall know the truth and the truth shall set you free. The bible says that the spirit of Christ is the spirit of liberty. Galatians 3: 28: There is neither jew nor greek, there is neither bond nor free, there is neither male nor female: for ye are all one in Christ Jesus. Ephesians 6:8: Knowing that whatsoever good thing any man doeth, the same shall he receive of the Lord, whether he be bond or free. Colossians 3: 11: Where there is neither Greek nor Jew, circumcision nor uncircumcision, Barbarian, Scythian, bond nor free: but Christ is all, and in all. 2nd Corinthians 3: 17: Now the Lord is that Spirit: and where the Spirit of the Lord is, there is liberty. We as Christians should know the mind of the Lord which is the word of God. He instructs us because we have made him Lord and are obedient unto him as we humble ourselves so that he can talk to us and instruct us. We have the mind of Christ as the bible says in the book of 1st Corinthians Chapter 2: verse 10: But God hath revealed them unto us by his spirit: for the spirit searcheth all things, yea, the deep things of God. Then if we were bound then we could not receive what the Holy Spirit wants to show us. All we have to do is repent of our sins unto God in the name of Jesus with a sincere heart and he will at that time forgive and pardon us of all our sins. In the book of 3rd John 1: verse 2: Beloved, I wish above all things that thou mayest prosper and be in health, even as thy soul prospereth. So we can prosper in every area of our lives as our minds prosper because our soul is the mind, will, and emotions which is the Self Analysis Character

Identification Code: The Sensory-Mechanism. The soul is also the belly area of man the body area where the Holy Spirit dwells in. An example of that is in the book of Matthew Chapter 16: verses 13-16. 13. When Jesus came into the coasts of Caesarea Philippi, he asked his disciples, saying, whom do men say that I the son of man am? 14. And they said, some say that thou art John the Baptist: some, Elias; and others, Jeremias, or one of the prophets. 15. He saith unto them, but whom say ye that I am? 16. And Simon Peter answered and said, thou art the Christ, the son of the living God. The Holy Spirit which is the Holy Ghost are angels. They are replicas of the Spirit of the Lord. These angels come to inhabit our lives. They come to strengthen, and to empower us. They come to lead, guide, and to direct us into all truth for Gods purpose. Matthew Chapter 16: verse 17: And Jesus answered and said unto him, Blessed art thou, Simon barjona: for flesh and blood hath not revealed it unto thee, but my Father which is in heaven. 18. And I say also unto thee, that thou art Peter, and upon this rock I will build my church; and the gates of hell shall not prevail against it. 19. And I will give unto thee the keys of the kingdom of heaven: and whatsoever thou shalt bind on earth shall be bound in heaven: and whatsoever thou shalt loose on earth shall be loosed in heaven.

Key point# 19:
(Flesh and blood); your soul, will, emotions, intellect, nor physical-body cannot reveal unto you who Jesus

Christ is but only God. God is Jesus Christ in the flesh. When you begin to discover who you are in Christ then the wrong people will leave your life because they will think that you are crazy. Anytime you have an encounter with Christ he changes your name from what was unto who you now become. Your rock is your faith in God. God is not looking for Mr. Perfect, or Ms. Perfect. God is looking for a humble people to use as a divine-instrument for his purpose. God don't have to choose you. He chooses to use you. God will use you to build his church by reshaping people and community's lives. The gate of hell is satan and his fallen-angels, demons, and unclean-spirits. The keys of the kingdom of heaven are Holy Angels which are the Holy Spirit the Holy Ghost. The mysteries, revelation, insight of Gods' way of doing things. Whatsoever you shall bind on earth which is your mind by prayer and action shall be bound in heaven which is your mind then your outer experience. Whatsoever you shall loose on earth which is your mind by prayer and action shall be loosed in heaven which is your mind then your outer experience. The gates of hell shall not prevail against us because we know Gods voice and the devil and his army cannot prevail against us. No weapon formed against you shall prosper.

Key point # 20:
Isaiah 54: 17: No weapon that is formed against thee shall prosper; and every tongue that shall rise against thee in judgment thou shalt condemn. This is the heritage of

the servants of the Lord, and their righteousness is of me, saith the Lord. Remember that the weapons will form but the scripture says that those weapons shall not prosper. Threats will not and shall not prosper if you stand on Gods' word. They will form but they will not prosper. God allows the weapons of the devil to come against you because he know that you can handle the attacks.

For whatsoever is born of God overcometh the world. 1st John Chapter 5: verses 4-5: 4. For whatsoever is born of God overcometh the world: and this is the victory that overcometh the world, even our faith. 5. Who is he that overcometh the world, but he that believeth that Jesus is the son of God? Apocalypse which is the anti- Christ shall come from the past. He is a clone. A fallen- angel. Remember that God cursed the fallen-angels yet again from being intimate with human-beings. These fallen-angels were with God in heaven and were given gifts from God. For the giftings and callings of God are without repentance. (The rise: of apocalypse): This being is so super-advanced that the scripture saith that the Holy Spirit won't let him be revealed yet but he's coming very soon. This angel's gift is time but he cannot use time to its fullest potential until Christ comes and takes the church back with him, because we know Gods voice we can decree what God has already said in his word as we listen to his voice which is the Holy Spirit. When I put in key number point number 20: about (apocalypse); this angels ability is time. This angel has the ability to transport from past, present, and future but cannot change them. Only to observe, watch, and to see what was, what is, and that which is to come. But the anti-Christ is already here. I have a group on my http://www.dynasty7.spruz.com and on my yahoo groups called mystery: of: iniquity: https://groups.yahoo.com/groups/mysteryofiniquity/ this fallen-angel is a shape-shifter. This angel is a master-mind. This angel is more advanced than satan. Satan is not so strong. He satan is only crafty and very influential. That's why when satan and his angels get cast into the lake of fire all the other fallen-angels, demons, and unclean-spirits are going to violently attack satan for letting him deceive them. There are angels who are more advanced than satan and they are ready to take satan out when it's time. These fallen-angels are subject unto satan until they are all cast into the lake of fire. Why are these angels subject unto satan? They are subject unto satan because the earth was already his. So in the rebellion God cast satan back to the earth and stripped him and the fallen angels of their anointing. Satan shall be tormented by these fallen-angels, demons, and unclean-spirits; forever, world without end.

Chapter 6

The Morning-Star: Power Over the Nations

Equinox, Time-Voules, Millennium, Quazar, Angel, Rod: of Iron. Revelation Chapter 2: verses 26-29: 26. And he that overcometh, and keepeth my works unto the end, to him will I give power over the nations: 27. And he shall rule them with a rod of iron; as the vessels of a potter shall they be broken to shivers: even as I received of my father. 28. And I will give him the morning star. 29. He that hath an ear, let him hear what the spirit saith unto the churches. Prophecy the final frontier. These are the voyages of the servants of God to boldly go where no man has gone before. Its mission to explore the purpose of life that God has predestined for mankind. One thing that Jesus stated in the book of John Chapter 16: verse 33: These things I have spoken unto you, that in me ye might have peace. In the world ye shall have tribulation: but be of good cheer; I have overcome the world. As long as we are here on this earth there will be trials, tests, and tribulations. The only trials, tests, and tribulations that you will ever face in life is what you allow to entertain you in your mind in your consciousness. The subconscious is the wife and the conscious is the husband. For where two are three are gathered together in the name of the Lord there is he in the midst of them. Both minds on one accord with Gods minds. Tests are given unto us to develop us, to mold, shape, and train, us into mastery. It's an open-book test to take us unto the next level. With new levels come new devils, as the bible says that we are changed from glory to glory. Jesus said that in him we might have peace to go through these tests with ease so that the tests won't affect us. The shalom peace of God is what we all need. It's a mantel of covering. So many people let the world dictate to them to bow down to the devils–system rather than overcoming the tests. There are 3 types of people that you will meet in life. Number 1. Those who think about succeeding. Number 2. Those who think about succeeding and try and quit after the first time. Number 3. those who not only think about overcoming and being successful, but when they fail they try, and try again until they succeed. As a man of God one who has been chosen and selected the devil is constantly throwing weapons of attacks at me, but as I overcome the system of the devil the gates of hell cannot prevail, nor stop me from fulfilling my destiny that God has predestined for me to do. Jesus said in the book Matthew Chapter 13: verses 11-12: 11. He answered and said unto them, because it is given unto you to know the mysteries of the kingdom of heaven, but to them it is not given. 12. For whosoever hath, to him shall be given, and he shall have more abundance: but whosoever hath not, from him shall be taken away even that he hath. Only a select few Christians receive the Mysteries of the Kingdom of Heaven. These mysteries are mainly for those who are in the five-fold known as preachers. The apostle, prophet, pastor, teacher, and evangelist which are all the ministry of helps to build Gods Kingdom. These functioning entities are for the perfecting of the saints of God for the grooming and maturing of Gods people. As you overcome tests God gives you power over the nations. God gives you power over the demonic-world that has men and women possessed and oppressed. They are known, as the demoniacs, devils, which are called demons. The bible says whatsoever you shall bind on earth shall be bound in heaven. And whatsoever you shall loose on earth shall be loosed in heaven. The living bible says and whatsoever we allow to happen here on earth he will allow to happen in heaven. And whatsoever we don't allow to happen here on earth he won't allow to happen in heaven. And a thousand years with the Lord is as a day. Time is winding down for the return of Jesus Christ the son of the living God. That's why Satan since the year 2010 has been allowed to upgrade his game. He's been allowed to increase his warfare and strategy. The reason why satan has been allowed to increase in his warfare is because you have people praying to him and other Gods thus empowering the devil to have some power. Jesus has all power as stated in the book of Matthew Chapter 28: verse 18: And Jesus came and spake unto them, saying, all power is given unto me in heaven and in earth. Let's observe and look at these notes in key point # 21: This is a prophetic-strategy:

Key Point # 21:

The morning star gives a person power over the nations to rule them with the word of God. Let me get one thing straight this is not witchcraft if you're using prayer for Gods purpose. For Gods will only. Witchcraft is the perversion of that which is good. Using something to manipulate someone for your own selfish gain is not of God. Power over the nation which means that Gods wants his people saved, delivered, and healed. So prayer causes angels to move on your behalf. In that which would have taken years for a person to do God does it in one day. As the bible says that a day with the Lord is as a thousand years.

Matthew 28:1, Christ's resurrection is declared by an angel to the women; Mt 28:9, he himself appears unto them; Matthew 28:11, the chief priests give the soldiers money to say that he was stolen out of his sepulchre; mat 28:16, Christ appears to his disciples, Mt 28:18. and sends them to baptize and teach all nations. We see in the book of Matthew Chapter 28: verse 1: Christ resurrection and an angel of God appeared to a woman. A. The prophetic word is the seed of God and must go through a pregnancy state. Prophecy must be handled with the gentle and care of the characteristics of a woman as if she's pregnant. Anytime you receive a word of the Lord an angel of God is there to assist you. B. In Matthew Chapter 28: verse 9: Christ appears. Since Christ is the head of the church and the husband is the head over his wife in the order that God has arranged it to be then prophecy 2nd stage becomes the man. The male who guards his pregnant wife. Instruction comes with the word of the Lord as Christ gave Mary Magdalene and the other Mary instruction to go tell the disciples to meet him in Galilee. You will be tested with the word of the Lord. Stewardship. C. In Matthew Chapter 28: verses 11-15: The devil will try and steal the word of the Lord from you, because satan know that the word of God will not come back void but will accomplish that which God send it. D. In the book of Matthew Chapter 28: verse 16-18: as you obey the word of the Lord Christ your manifestation appears. The word of the Lord will come to pass and pass into your direction as you're obedient. E. In the prophetic word there is power over the nations as Christ said teaching all nations to observe all things which I have commanded you. God gives you wisdom, knowledge, and understanding in the word of the Lord. In the book of Isaiah Chapter 52: verses 12-15: 12. For ye shall not go out with haste, nor go by flight: for the Lord will go before you; and the God of Israel will be your reward. 13. Behold, my servant shall deal prudently, he shall be exalted and extolled, and be very high. 14. As many were astonied at thee; his visage was so marred more than any man, and his form more than the sons of men: 15. So shall he sprinkle many nations; the kings shall shut their mouths at him: for that which had not been told them shall they see; and that which they had not heard shall they consider. In that which would have taken years for you to do God will do it through you in 1 day. People judge and criticize because they don't know what they are talking about. A lot of times it's jealously because of who you are in Christ. I heard the Master prophet Bishop Jordan say in Cosmic-Economics that people don't have a problem with what you do. They have to problem with who you have become. God promised that he would go before us and be our reward. He promised us that he would cause us to deal prudently. That God would exalt us and promote us. Even in our own problems and situations God will promote us. He would cause our enemies and the whole world to see a new transformation that would cause them to acknowledge that he has loved us. The bible says that in the book of Isaiah Chapter 45: verse 1-3: 1. Thus saith the Lord to his anointed, to Cyrus, whose right hand I have holden, to subdue nations before him; and I will loose the loins of kings, to open before him the two leaved gates; and the gates shall not be shut; 2. I will go before thee, and make the crooked places straight: I will break in pieces the gates of brass, and cut in sunder the bars of iron: 3. And I will give thee the treasures of darkness, and hidden riches of secret places, that thou mayest know that I, the Lord, which call thee by thy name, am the God of Israel. God said that he would be our reward which basically says that whatever the devil stole from you God would restore sevenfold. I saw years ago around about the year 2001 a dream of me being exalted in the air with the finest apparel and I was very high in the air with the glory of God all on me. This dream was God talking to me that it would surely come to pass in my life. Dreams and visions are messages. Dreams are more literal and visions are more pictorial. In the book of Isaiah Chapter 46: verse 10: Declaring the end from the beginning, and from ancient times the things that are not yet done, saying, my counsel shall stand, and I will do all my pleasure: This scripture is saying that do things the way God wants to do them. He created it so he can do as he pleases. Prophecy at its first stage is a seed. It's a word that is fluorescent in the darkness.

Key Point # 22:

My mentor Bishop Jordan always says that the prophetic-word of God is a gift of revelation enabling you to walk into the fullness of Gods destiny for your life. The prophetic-word speaks death to your past, but speaks life to your future. If there is a lack of provision then check your vision through the eyes of prophecy. Which means Isaiah Chapter 43: verses 18- 19: 18. Remember ye not the former things, neither consider the things of old. 19. Behold, I will do a new thing; now it shall spring forth; shall ye not know it? I will even make a way in the wilderness, and rivers in the desert. In dreams and visions Gods shows us the end from the beginning based on our faith which causes us to stand. God shows and reveals unto us the end from the beginning so that we may hold on unto the promises despite all the obstacles and tests we must pass in order to receive the manifestation.

Key Point # 23:

Manifestation is a man at their station. For if you do not know who you are assigned too then you're off track. For a double-minded man is unstable in all his ways. The manifestation which is the miracle should already been inside of you. For as a man or a mind thinketh in his heart so is he. As my mentor Bishop Jordan always say that we must marry a mind. The marital union of thought.

God chooses the foolish things of this world to confound the wise by causing us to deal prudently which is wisdom. Intelligence can be a tool of the devil which is knowledge if you don't apply wisdom unto it. The scripture says that in the book of Matthew Chapter 7: verses 24-27: 24. Therefore whosoever heareth these sayings of mine, and doeth them, I will liken him unto a wise man, which built his house upon a rock: 25. And the rain descended, and the floods came, and the winds blew, and beat upon that house; and it fell not: for it was founded upon a rock. 26. And every one that heareth these sayings of mine, and doeth them not, shall be likened unto a foolish man, which built his house upon the sand: 27. And the rain descended, and the floods came, and the winds blew, and beat upon that house; and it fell: and great was the fall of it. When God said that he will liken us unto a wise man he is saying that he will take us out of obscurity and set us on high above all the nations of the earth. God will set us very high because we are in his hand. God allows us to be separated from people so that they can't contaminate us, nor pollute us. Isaiah Chapter 49: verses 7-8: 7. Thus saith the Lord, the redeemer of Israel, and his holy one, to him whom man despiseth, to him whom the nation abhorreth, to a servant of rulers, kings shall see and arise, princes also shall worship, because of the Lord that is faithful, and the holy one of Israel, and he shall choose thee. 8. Thus saith the Lord, in an acceptable time have I heard thee, and in a day of salvation have I helped thee: and I will preserve thee, and give thee for a covenant of the people, to establish the earth, to cause to inherit the desolate heritages; In my earlier years in ministry a lot of people despised and rejected me because they said that I did not fit in. Some of them didn't have to say a word because I could see the hatred, rage, and envy on their faces. Ezekiel Chapter 3: verse 8: Behold, I have made thy face strong against their faces, and thy forehead strong against their foreheads. In those earlier years in ministry I did not understand at the time that the Lord was about to use me by separating me for a special purpose. At that time I did not know that the Lord had called and chosen me as an apostle. But as I served in the church and I was tried and elevated as a deacon. After a few years I was elevated unto a prophet, but after I was violently casted out of the church for no reason it was that the Lord revealed to me that I was an apostle. God will use peoples weaknesses to prepare you for your destiny, but you must forgive. Remember that if you are called into the apostle-ship you must first walk as a prophet then God will elevate you into an apostle. The scripture says in Isaiah Chapter 52: So shall he sprinkle many nations. The reason why you will sprinkle many nations is because all of the hell, trials, tests, tribulations, rejections, and betrayals that you have been through. I heard Bishop T.D. jakes say many times on the Potters House Broadcast that rejection is good; that his enemies did more for him by betraying, hurting, lying, and rejecting him because it made him into the awesome man of God that he is today. God bless you Bishop Jakes, oh yes they have a lot to talk about and so do I. God didn't save you just for nothing. God saved you because he loved you. He saved you so that he may use you for his purpose so that you can help other people. Many people say over and over again that they don't know what is there purpose and the scripture says in the book of acts Chapter 1: verse 8: But ye shall receive power, after that the Holy Ghost is come upon you: and ye shall be witnesses unto me both in Jerusalem, and in all Judaea, and in Samaria, and unto the uttermost part of the earth. We are here to be witnesses for the Lord Jesus Christ. Even if you don't know what God has called and chosen for you to be know that you are here on this earth to be a witness. Fast for 3 days and seek the Lord in prayer and he will reveal to you your purpose in life. The kings shall shut their mouths at him because God has given you a lot of wisdom, knowledge, and understanding throughout the years. That's why the bible says that in the book of Jeremiah Chapter 3: verse 15: And I will give you pastors according to mine heart, which shall feed you with knowledge and understanding. The morning-star gives a person power to live the life that God has predestined for you before the foundation of the world. I have had many dreams of me personally traveling around the world talking to people. The Lord showed me the end from the beginning. The real you is a spirit and not your physical body. The bible says that in the book of Genesis Chapter 1: verse 26: And God said, let us make man in our image, after our likeness: and let them have dominion over the fish of the sea, and over the fowl of the air, and over the cattle, and over all the earth, and over every creeping thing that creepeth upon the earth. Jesus said in the book of John Chapter 4: verse 24: God is a spirit: and they that worship him must worship him in spirit and in truth. God is a spirit. When we worship God in spirit and in truth. He's saying that we must serve him in his divinity as God almighty. Spirit is God. Truth is the son. Even though God is the son and the son is God. Christ is spirit and God is also truth. You can't have one without the other. God can use any form. The prophetic word was spoken before God came to earth in the form of a man. The manifestation of the prophecy manifested here in the earth. Spirit is the word that was and is spoken. Manifestation is spirit in physical-form. When your physical-body dies it returns back to the ground, while your spirit-man returns back unto God. You choice heaven or the lake of fire. God will share his glory with no man. The glory goes unto God and that no flesh should glory in his presence. He is a jealous God visiting the iniquities of the fathers unto the third and fourth generation. Jesus said that the gates of hell shall not prevail which I said earlier that the gates of hell are the system of the devil composed of satan, who is the devil, fallen-angels known, as princes over principalities. Principalities are the territories, land, place where these princes reside over. Demons are the offspring of fallen-angels and human-beings, demons are the nephalim which are giants. People say they saw big-foot and they were not lying. Since demons are the nephalim giants therefore these demons are half human and half angel. So they have some dominion ship here in the earth realm. They can appear from time to time. Unclean spirits are the souls of those who never confessed Jesus Christ as their Lord and savior. These are those who are evil and wicked and are slaves of the devil, sickness, disease, illnesses are from unclean spirits. That's why before you move into an apartment, home, or trailer anoint your place of residence with oil and cast those evil spirit out of that place in which you reside in so that the peace of God may reside with you there. For we wrestle not against flesh and blood but against principalities, fallen-angels, powers which is their authority against the rulers of darkness of this world.

There are many people who are possessed and possessed by the demonic. Remember in the book of Daniel Chapter 10: when Gabriel told Daniel that you're beloved of God. And that from the moment you prayed God heard you, but the prince of Persia withstood me twenty and one days. The price of Persia was a man and the spirit (principality) working through that man was the devil. There are many people who are being influence by the demonic-world. It's called demonic-influence. Against spiritual wickedness in high places. The spiritual wickedness is witchcraft, manipulation, and seduction. Witchcraft is also the pharmaceuticals, known as medicine drugs to manipulate and to control people for the use to make money. Not every pharmaceutical is bad; however the majority of pharmaceuticals are witchcraft. The high place is the mind, the central-head-quarters of operations, the consciousness, the subconscious is also the spirit, the blood has life in it which is the spirit, the consciousness is like the flesh or physical body. The carnal nature of man is the sensory-mechanism. I heard Dr. Creflo Dollar called the consciousness the sensory-mechanism. He was teaching years ago about spiritual-bumpers and he was speaking about comparing the consciousness to the sensory-mechanism which is the five-senses. The bible says that we are not ignorant of the satans devices which are his strategies. The devices of the devil are the works of the flesh. To get us out of the will of God to get us out of spirit unto the will of self. The reason why the gates of hell shall not prevail is because of what God has said in his word. What God has personally told you that sets you high above all the nations of the earth. Angels can teleport from door to door because they are spirit. We as human-beings are spirit also. Ezekiel Chapter 21: verses 25-27: 25. And thou, profane wicked prince of Israel, whose day is come, when iniquity shall have an end, 26. Thus saith the Lord God; remove the diadem, and take off the crown: this shall not be the same: exalt him that is low, and abase him that is high 27. I will overturn, overturn, overturn, it: and it shall be no more, until he come whose right it is; and I will give it him.

Key Point # 24:
Yea I hear the word of the Lord saying that I am shaking the heavens and the earth. For this is the time and season of 7 years of plenty. and in 2020 will begin the 7 years of famine. For I am changing things in a miraculous way. I am removing the wicked out of power. I am showing them that man shall not live by bread alone, but by every word of the mouth of God. I am raising up my trained soldiers in many facets. I am doing a new thing in 2013-2020. In these 7 years I am causing my power to be shed abroad all over the word. I am placing my people in positions that will cause their enemies to be shocked, amazed, and to acknowledge that I have loved them. I am opening up my voice through my chosen- saints to prepare the way for the coming of the Lord. My saints shall say they are the voice of one crying in the wilderness prepare the way

of the Lord. New governments shall arise and emerge. yea, destruction is coming; great destruction shall come swiftly after the 7 years saith the Lord. These will be times in 2020 where my word shall seem to be scare and void, but not so saith the Lord. The nations shall run to hear what is the word of the Lord. They shall no more run unto the dry deceitful tress. But they shall run unto my trees that I have chosen. In 2020 there will be massive opposition coming against my body saith the Lord. Then shall false Christ come and shall show deceitful signs and lying wonders. As this will be the species to begin to walk upon the earth. Clones shall begin to come upon the scenes a great, evil wickedness is on the rise in the year 2020. My glory shall not only be in the churches saith the Lord but I am giving my faithful servants double for their trouble in these 7 years. Governments shall seek my servant's advice and help like never before. Great and terrible visions are coming to the great leaders in these 7 years; I am bringing my servants out of the pit into majesty. The 1st shall be last and the last shall be first. There will be signs in these 7 years saith the Lord of the removal of my holy word, but not yet. These are just the beginning of birth pains. The rise of the economic collapse is already happening, but my people shall have plenty and more than enough saith the spirit of almighty God. I had an experience with an angel one night as I was standing in the back of a church. I asked the Lord out loud to manifest himself to me and as I was walking back into the church I heard a loud, terrible, awesome sound of an explosion and I looked up and I saw fire. I saw clouds enfolding itself as described in the book of Ezekiel Chapter one. The fire was separate from the clouds. They merged and joined together. And I saw a huge, giant, tall light–blue angel that looked like a cartoon character and he smiled and waved at me. He was dressed in armor like a roman soldier. I remember that I told the pastor and other clergy of the church and they were in awe. I remember one day when I was at my mother house that as I was about to cross the street that I saw a black truck pull up to the stop sign on opposite of me on the left and there was a very tall angel in the truck that looked like a man, and the glory of God was all on him all over his body. And he had on a black jacket, and he looked at me with total amazement. He looked shocked and he took off in the truck fast as the speed of lighting and the cars on the left side of the road as he got off the right side of the road stopped. The cars stopped as he took off as the speed of lighting. And the people immediately got out of their cars in such shock and amazement, and they were trying to figure out what was moving so fast. I mean these people were very shocked. The Kingdom has been placed inside of each and every one of us as saved born again believers and, as Jesus said in the book of Luke Chapter 17: verses 20-21: 20. And when he was demanded of the Pharisees, when the kingdom of God should come, he answered them and said, the kingdom of God cometh not with observation: 21. Neither shall they say, lo here! or, lo there! for, behold, the kingdom of God is within you. Remember that the kingdom of God is the power of God. Now the kingdom of heaven is a place, realm, and dimension which is the realm of the spirit. The morning-star is the spirit of God the paracletes. Angels are replicas of the spirit of the Lord. The spirit of the Lord is what's protecting us in the earth. The spirit of the Lord is shielding us. The kingdom of God is the spirit of the Lord. The spirit of the Lord is also the kingdom of Heaven. The kingdom of God is the morning-star. Satan who used to be lucifer was the son of the morning as stated in the book of Isaiah Chapter 14: verse 12: How art thou fallen from heaven, o Lucifer, son of the morning! how art thou cut down to the ground, which didst weaken the nations! That's why the scripture says in the book of revelation Chapter 22: verse 16: I Jesus have sent mine angel to testify unto you these things in the churches. I am the root and the offspring of David, and the bright and morning star. God being the root and offspring of David is his divinity as a perfect sinless man. He is the author and finisher of our faith. He is the son of man. The supreme divine ruler of the universe God almighty. And he says that he is the bright and morning star. God will never leaves his throne. His spirit which is the spirit of the Lord or the spirit of God is God himself in action without leaving his throne. Satan who is the son of the morning rebelled against God who is the bright and morning-star. God who is Jehovah is greater than all. Even as a sinful man God gave satan the advantage and satan still miserable failed time after time again. The power that God has in stored in you which is the Holy

Ghost operates from within you, because these keys represent different levels of anointings. Jesus said that in the book of John Chapter 14: verse 2: In my father's house are many mansions: if it were not so, I would have told you. I go to prepare a place for you. This scripture and verse is an exact confirmation of exodus Chapter 23: verse 20: not only will we receive homes, and different levels of anointings', but God was talking about us having a new body that this corruptible body shall be gone and that he would give us an incorruptible body. Adam had immortality before he fell from grace.

Key Point # 25:

The morning-star is the ability after overcoming trails, tests, and tribulation's to change time which is seasons. To unlock all scripture, control nations; its power that God gives you to do his work which he has called as an established order and principle here on earth. Remember as I stated earlier not to manipulate people but God gives us the power of prayer to set the captives free. Power that when you have overcome the trials, tests, and tribulations of that season to move into another season. When God says that he will never leave you nor forsake you he's saying that he is the morning-star. That he is all power and that he has given us all power to do what he has called and chosen for us to do here in the earth-realm.

A primary example in the book of Jeremiah Chapter 52: verses 12-15: that which would have taken you years to do God will do it in you in one day. The power is not in the White House, nor in the Judicial-System, nor in our Government, nor in our Military, but in God A mighty. The power is in God the supreme, divine, ruler, of the universe. The power is in those who believe in the Lord Jesus Christ that God has raised him from the dead and that he sits on the right hand of the father. The white-house is supposed to be set up like a spiritual Israel because our government was set up on biblical-principles. There was a woman who took prayer out of school and she was successful at this. This woman did not do this by herself. She had multitudes of people in her ear and she wanted to be the one to get this done. These are jezebel's eunuchs. Jezebels workers. Remember that the jezebel spirit can operate in male or female, but mainly operates in females. Witches can be male or females; but wherever there is a jezebel there will also be the warlock. The warlock name is in the book of Exodus Chapter 7: verse 1: And the Lord said unto Moses, see I have made thee a God to Pharaoh: and Aaron thy brother shall be thy prophet. The warlock is the pharaoh-spirit. The warlock-spirit can only operate in a male it cannot operate in a female. The highest jezebel spirit there is which is the warlock. a.k.a. pharaoh because the order cannot change. God ordained the male to be over his wife and not the wife to be over her husband. That doesn't mean that the male should control, torture, nor beat his wife. The wife has to come under her husband because she is submitted unto the Lord Jesus Christ and the husband is submitted to the Lord Jesus Christ as well. Husbands ought to love their wives as Christ loved the church. There are many warlocks in the churches and in the world. God is about to expose these false shepherds and remove them out of power. They are set in the churches to try and stop, and block the move of God. No one can stop, nor block or hinder the move of God. God is a patient and desires that no man perish but all come to repentance. I had a dream years ago and my family were in the house and we were joking around, then we all went outside slowly and we saw some brown tall grass and something was moving through the grass and we couldn't see what it was that was moving then we saw a creature that looked like a character in a movie that Jim Henson had made called the Dark Crystal. It was one of the creatures that had his life taken away from them by those big vultures and my family screamed and they took off running while I was still standing in peace, the creature looked like a worm. Next the creature looked shocked and amazed. When I woke up that morning I prayed that God would reveal to me what the dream meant; the Lord told me and gave me this scripture. Micah Chapter 7: verses 15-17: 15. According to the days of thy coming out of the land of Egypt will I shew unto him marvelous things. 16. The nations shall see and be confounded at all their might: they shall lay their hand upon their mouth, their ears shall be deaf. 17. They shall lick the dust like a serpent, they shall move out of their holes like worms of the earth: they shall be afraid of the Lord our God, and shall fear because of thee. So the Lord gave me the revelation and I had peace about the dream. I wrote a poem in the 9th grade at La Marque high school and I remember the teacher that I had for English, he taught us like we were in college and the poem went like this equinox, time-voules, millennium crucibly dining in eternal hell giving up one's life in exchange for another one is truly, truly a hellifying experience. Even from a child I knew that hell was a real reality, as well as heaven. Just as the bible says that the giftings and the callings of God are without repentance. So even those of you who are not saved have gifts that have made a way for some of you, but without the Lord Jesus Christ they will not prosper righteously.

Key Point # 26:

When Jesus gave Peter the keys of the kingdom of heaven he gave Peter which is the rock the morning-star. God restored dominion ship back unto him, not because of his own works but because of his faith. That's why Jesus said that flesh and blood did not reveal this to you, but my father which is in heaven. Heaven means spirit. Prophets have the uncanny-supernatural ability to separate flesh and blood from spirit. It was not of Peters owns works that caused God to move on his behalf. It was because Peter knew who Christ was. In your life when you are going through trials, tests, and tribulations your revelation of who God is will cause you to triumph and to overcome that season of your life. When you get a revelation of who God is then you walk into a wilderness to be tempted by the devil, but it is by your faith in God that you get a revelation of who he is and God is the Christ; God in human-form.

Chapter 7

Write the Vision and make it plain

To each and everybody that has a dream or vision then you have just stepped into the order and process of planning and organization. Proverbs Chapter 29: verse 18: Where there is no vision, the people perish: but he that keepeth the law, happy is he. in the book of Habakkuk Chapter 2: verses 2-3: 2 And the Lord answered me, and said, write the vision, and make it plain upon tables, that he may run that readeth it. 3. For the vision is yet for an appointed time, but at the end it shall speak, and not lie: though it tarry, wait for it; because it will surely come, it will not tarry. We are unusual people that must write the promises and things of God down. So in the book of Joshua Chapter 1: verse 8: we must meditate think continually upon the word of God. So that we may observe to do what God wants us to do. So that we may prosper and be successful in the things of God and whatsoever you think about long enough becomes an image in your mind and that image becomes an imagination that starts to change the season that you are in. for as he thinketh in his heart so is he. We are whatsoever we mediate from within our hearts. God gave us the same principal that he used in creation. For if we focus long enough on the desire and confess it our whole world changes. When a person acts on their imagination it then becomes a reality. a.k.a. the universal-remote. I have a group http://www. dynasty7.spruz.com and I have the same group on my yahoo groups under the name cydnamonia@yahoo. com called Universal-Remote: The Power: of: Prayer. We must down our dreams and visions from the Lord in a journal so that we can plain. Organization is critical and is key to the manifestation of the desire from God. Therefore we can have organization to take us into the direction that God wants us to go towards and God gave Habakkuk a vision and the only way he could see the vision he has to work Gods principle by writing it down. So that he can meditate on it while being patient for it will surely come to pass. Just like God told Joshua to meditate upon the word of God say and night while observing the vision. I have so many dream journals since the end of 1999 and this book that you are reading dreams and visions: the expressed, inspired, secret revelations: of God: volume 1: is only one of a lot of books that I have been inspired to write. And I have been writing all of my dreams and visions along with words that the Lord told me about that day to confirm them. Things that are about to come. For dream and vision interpretation ask the Lord to give you the anointing to interpret dreams and visions and he will give it unto you or go to a class where they are teaching about dream and vision interpretation. People in today's society write their schedules down to keep them organized for their tasks and the world is successful to an extent; however we as believers in Christ are supposed to prosper far greater that; because we are Gods children his sons and daughters. We should write down our dreams and visions that the Lord has given us as we do our assignments. It is the way that God planned for us to do. Schedules are very important, for instance when you're at your work place you may have to clock in, or sign in on a time sheet which guides and direct you successfully through the day. Such as lunch break and other ventures of that work day. I worked at H.E.B. in Galveston in 1998 until the year 2000, and we had schedules. We had to clock in on a time sheet when we came into work and we had to clock out on a time sheet when we left work. So it is of great importance for us to have schedules which are an established principle, the first five books of the bible is commonly called by theologians the Pentateuch which was written by Moses or the law of Moses. That all the children of Israel had to follow and do. The Egyptians used paper that was called papyrus to write things down. They also used papyrus to draw things down. Papyrus was a great system back then and we have a system called paper we used notebooks, journals, folders, binders. Now we have Microsoft word, open office and much more to organize our thoughts. Not only the Egyptians had a system but many cultures and civilizations used so form of instrument to put their writings on. King Solomon who was the wisest man in his time until Jesus came did a lot of writing and one of his most common popular books that he ever wrote was the book of proverb, which has a lot of wisdom even for today's times. Jesus in the book of Revelation told John to write to the seven churches. John was meditating on what Jesus was telling him about visions as we talked about earlier is a project of the kingdom of God that he wants established here on the earth. Thy kingdom come thy will be done on earth as it is in heaven. I use to have about three to four dreams that I wrote down in my dream journals. So that I could meditate on them as well also prophesy the promised into existence. Another reason why you should write your dreams and visions down is because so that the devil cant steal them from you.

Key point # 27:

You have to be very careful who you share your information with, because everyone who says they are for you are not for you. These are liars filthy dreamers who defile the flesh. Mockers, writing down your dreams and visions give you hope, increases your faith and gives your life despite what's going on around you. That's why we must at all times watch, listen, look, and very carefully observe our surrounding at all times. Matthew Chapter 7: verse 6: Give not that which is holy unto the dogs, neither cast ye your pearls before swine, lest they trample them under their feet, and turn again and rend you don't cast your secrets unto demons the devil doesn't know no more than what you tell him. Satan and his imps can also work through people in order to get close to you.

Whenever you are going through a trial, or you start doubting you can go back unto what God promised you as insurance. God said that his word will not return back unto him void. It will accomplish everything he sends it to do. In the book of numbers Chapter 23: verse 19: God is not a man, that he should lie; neither the son of man, that he should repent: hath he said, and shall he not do it? Or hath he spoken, and shall he not make it good? The mediation of your mind is so important that you become what you put into you. Remember that you just brought that product, whatever you do is the exact result of what you have installed into your Bio-Tech- Synchronization Center which is your mind. You have a record history database mechanism which is the mind, start writing down your dreams and visions as they are given unto you. We are visual people that have to see things to mix with our faith whether we are saved or not, but we who are believers in the Lord Jesus Christ can all see dreams and visions to a certain extent. The prophet can see into the spirit because of the grace of God, just because the spirit of prophecy falls on you does not make you a prophet. Who wants to be a prophet? They have to be out of their minds. Prophets are so rejected by people that they are constantly persecuted. The Holy Spirit will lead you what to say and what to write, because you are unleashing rivers of living waters out of your inner most being. God will allow his prophets and servants to suffer and to go through persecutions so that we don't get the big head. Jesus said that out of your belly shall low rivers of living waters. The answers of life will flow from within us. This is also the kingdom of God. These mysteries that God has placed in us before we ever came out of our mother's womb. In the book of Revelation Chapter 7: verses 15-17: 15. Therefore are they before the throne of God, and serve him day and night in his temple: and he that sitteth on the throne shall dwell among them. 16. They shall hunger no more, neither thirst anymore; neither shall the sun light on them, nor any heat. 17. For the lamb which is in the midst of the throne shall feed them, and shall lead them unto living fountains of waters: and God shall wipe away all tears from their eyes. All the wealth is inside of you and as you write down your dreams, and visions from the Lord you must plan. You must plan by seeking the Lord in prayer daily. Plan and process your imagination as you are led by the Holy Spirit. Whenever you hear people speaking negative know that this is a sign that the wealth inside of them is contaminated; therefore they can't receive from the Lord. Their vision is distorted which causes doubt to hider the manifestation of the blessing of God into their lives. Living fountains of waters in the book of Revelation was referring to God leading his people unto wealth, and total life prosperity. God will lead you unto status, recognition, and abundant resources. Say out loud that my mind has power because I have a mind just like God. 1st Corinthians Chapter 2: verse 16: For who hath known the mind of the Lord, that he may instruct him? But we have the mind of Christ, that's why we must renew our minds daily. So many people are too lazy to renew their minds; we must renew our minds daily with the word of God. You must not allow the past to hold you back in natural. Write down your prayer requests and pray over them daily. If you look up the word prayer it means speech. death and life are in the power of the tongue. And they that love it shall eat the fruit thereof. Prophesy over your life daily. Command your day and so shall it be. Your angels are ready for your command, purchase what Gods word says about you by marrying the mind of God. Remember that the mind is the central headquarters of operations; that you are no more than what you see yourself to be. Whatsoever you pay attention too will attract unto you. You must see yourself through the eyes of God, because God only sees himself. That's why God asked Adam in the book of Genesis Chapter 3: verse 9: And the Lord God called unto Adam, and said unto him, where art thou? God only sees himself which is you when you are walking in righteousness; right standing with God. Knowledge is obtainable and accessible and is of great value when it is used properly to declare the kingdom of God. Knowledge with wisdom produces understanding. Deuteronomy Chapter 8: verse 18: But thou shalt remember the Lord thy God: for it is he that giveth thee power to get wealth that he may establish his covenant which he sware unto thy fathers, as it is this day. God is saying that is it not our righteousness, or our good works that has given us wealth the abundant supply. It's because of his grace and mercy that we are joint heirs with Christ.. We should write down the dreams and visions that God give us, and we should meditate upon them daily until they manifest. There may be some of you who may be having a hard time focusing on the visions that God has given you. Start going on a fast as directed by the Lord, so that your body can shut down. So that you may listen unto the word of the Lord inside of you.

Key Point: # 28:
Fasting is when you shut yourself down in order to listen clearly unto the voice of God on the inside of you. You anoint yourself with oil and go on a fast as the Lord leads you to go on one.

There are many types of fasts. Fasting shuts down your mind, your intellect and removes junk, and strongholds from you. A lot of times God is speaking unto us and we cannot hear him. You can go on a three day fast, a week fast, two week fast, twenty one day fast, a month fast, thirty day fast, forty day fast as the Lord leads you to. You can eat fruits, salads, vegetables. Stay away from meats, and starches. Fasting flushes away things that are hindering you. Fasting releases toxins from your spirit and from your blood stream and you eat the word of God while your own your fast to empower you. You can also go on a water fast, just make sure the Lord directs you and not yourself. What types of fast should you go on? You pray and let the Lord direct you. You may want to go on an hour or more on your fast to start out. A lot of times when God have you to fast there is warfare about to break out, so God prepares you so that you may mount up with the wings of an eagle when the storm is over. Fasting also clears your mind, because the flesh and the mind will sometimes bring doubt. Which can hinder the spirit of God within you. But to those who want to go on longer fasts know of a surety that it works. Isaiah Chapter 58: verses 1-11: 1. Cry aloud, spare not, lift up thy voice like a trumpet, and shew my people their transgression, and the house of Jacob their sins. 2. Yet they seek me daily, and delight to know my ways, as a nation that did righteousness, and forsook not the ordinance of their God: they ask of me the ordinances of justice; they take delight in approaching to God. 3. Wherefore have we fasted, say they, and thou seest not? wherefore have we afflicted our soul, and thou takest no knowledge? behold, in the day of your fast ye find pleasure, and exact all your labours. 4. Behold, ye fast for strife and debate, and to smite with the fist of wickedness: ye shall not fast as ye do this day, to make your voice to be heard on high. 5. It is such a fast that I have chosen? a day for a man to afflict his soul? is it to bow down his head as a bulrush, and to spread sackcloth and ashes under him? wilt thou call this a fast, and an acceptable day to the Lord? 6. Is not this the fast that I have chosen? to loose the bands of wickedness, to undo the heavy burdens, and to let the oppressed go free, and that ye break every yoke? 7. Is it not to deal thy bread to the hungry, and that thou bring the poor that are cast out to thy house? when thou seest the naked, that thou cover him; and that thou hide not thyself from thine own flesh? 8. Then shall thy light break forth as the morning, and thine health shall spring forth speedily: and thy righteousness shall go before thee; the glory of the Lord shall be thy reward. 9. Then shalt thou call, and the Lord shall answer; thou shalt cry, and he shall say, here I am. if thou take away from the midst of thee the yoke, the putting forth of the finger, and speaking vanity; 10. And if thou draw out thy soul to the hungry, and satisfy the afflicted soul; then shall thy light rise in obscurity and thy darkness be as the noonday: 11. And the Lord shall guide thee continually, and satisfy thy soul in drought, and make fat thy bones: and thou shalt be like a watered garden, and like a spring of water, whose waters fail not. Fasting breaks and removes the yokes from us, also fasting cause's angels to come to our rescue. Fasting removes us from our will and brings us to do God's will. Fasting also causes healing and restorations in our spirit and soul and you can always go back and look at your dream and vision journal to remind you of what God has said to keep you confident despite opposition. I have a series of dream and visions journals that I have told you about that I have been writing since the year 1999. God bless you. May the

Lord bless thee, keep thee, be gracious unto thee, cause his face to shine upon thee, lift his countenance upon thee,and may the Lord give you and your love ones peace. Numbers Chapter 6: verses 24-26:

Chapter 8

The Universal-Key: of Spiritual Self-Mastery: Unlocking: the Master: Within

The master is the one who is inside of us the Holy Spirit. for greater is he that is in us than he that is in the world. my dependency for so long was in man. That was my down fall; I had to be pushed out of the nest. I felt betrayed, rejected, hurt, and much more; however rejection is a great thing it pushes you to a point that you need God like never before. Who is the master? Say I am the master. I know too many people they would say that's blasphemy, but scripture says in the book of Psalms Chapter 82: verse 6: I have said, ye are Gods; and all of you are children of the most high. We are all miniature Gods that have been placed here on this earth to do a job for the Lord. It's crazy how a lot of us were never told when we were younger who we are. Our parents didn't know any better, they wanted us to be doctors, lawyers, teachers, psychologist, and much more. That's why a lot of us have been wandering from job to job.

Many people never find what it is that fills their desire. I was ministering on a series on blogtalkradio.com in 2011 called sheep in the midst of wolves, and it's the story of Saul and the Lord's disciple Ananias. I recently did a similar series called the origin and mystery of the symbiote. And it's also dealing with Saul and the Lord's disciple Ananias how that Saul knew that he was a born leader he just stood out from among all the rest he knew the law he knew the word of God. But he did not have a relationship with God through Jesus Christ. Acts Chapter 9: verses 1-18: 1.And Saul, yet breathing out threatening's and slaughter against the disciples of the Lord, went unto the high priest, 2: And desired of him letters to Damascus to the synagogues, that if he found any of this way, whether they were men or women, he might bring them bound unto Jerusalem. 3. And as he journeyed, he came near Damascus: and suddenly there shined round about him a light from heaven: 4. And he fell to the earth, and heard a voice saying unto him, Saul, Saul, why persecutest thou me? 5. And he said, who art thou, Lord? and the Lord said, I am Jesus whom thou persecutest: it is hard for thee to kick against the pricks. 6. And he trembling and astonished said, Lord, what wilt thou have me to do? and the Lord said unto him, arise, and go into the city, and it shall be told thee what thou must do. 7. And the men which journeyed with him stood speechless, hearing a voice, but seeing no man. 8. And Saul arose from the earth; and when his eyes were opened, he saw no man: but they led him by the hand, and brought him into Damascus. 9.

And he was three days without sight, and neither did eat nor drink. 10. And there was a certain disciple at Damascus, named Ananias; and to him said the Lord in a vision, Ananias. and he said, behold, I am here, Lord. 11. And the Lord said unto him, arise, and go into the street which is called straight, and enquire in the house of Judas for one called Saul, of tarsus: for, behold, he prayeth, 12. And hath seen in a vision a man named Ananias coming in, and putting his hand on him, that he might receive his sight. 13. Then Ananias answered, Lord, I have heard by many of this man, how much evil he hath done to thy saints at Jerusalem: 14. And here he hath authority from the chief priests to bind all that call on thy name. 15. But the Lord said unto him, go thy way: for he is a chosen vessel unto me, to bear my name before the gentiles, and kings, and the children of Israel: 16. For I will shew him how great things he must suffer for my name's sake. 17. And Ananias went his way, and entered into the house; and putting his hands on him said, brother Saul, the Lord, even Jesus, that appeared unto thee in the way as thou camest, hath sent me, that thou mightest receive thy sight, and be filled with the Holy Ghost. 18. And immediately there fell from his eyes as it had been scales: and he received sight forthwith, and arose, and was baptized. Saul who after his conversion years later became the apostle Paul. He was persecuting Gods people. Saul knew he was a born leader from birth. He just stood out from all the rest. When Saul spoke everyone listened. His leadership was very expertise but he was using his leadership wrong.

On the road to Damascus a bright light shined from heaven which was an angel, and God spoke through the angel unto Saul. This was a point in which Saul's life would change for the better. The Lord asked Saul why are you persecuting me. And Saul asked the Lord what will you have me to do? Which lets you know that God had been speaking to Saul numerous times, but Saul kept running from the Lord. The church was behind the scenes praying against the persecution, and an angel of God was able to come forth. Saul was a master indeed but he was very corrupt. 1st Timothy Chapter 1: verse 13: Who was before a blasphemer, and a persecutor, and injurious: but I obtained mercy, because I did it ignorantly in unbelief. The apostle Paul gave an account before his conversion how he was persecuting Gods people ignorantly. God spare him because he thought that he was doing the will of God.

Key point # 29:

There are many people who are going in the wrong direction whom the Lord is about to visit. In these next 7 years from 2013 to 2020 there will be a lot of angelic-visitations. A lot of people do not know that they are persecuting Gods people. We are about to see in these 7 year period a lot of conversions. Several people in the world are about to confess Jesus Christ as their personal Lord and savior. The shift is about to happen. We are about to see actresses, celebrities, movie stars, sport stars, rich and wealthy people converting. Ezekiel Chapter 36: verses 24-27: 24. For I will take you from among the heathen, and gather you out of all countries, and will bring you into your own land. 25. Then will I sprinkle clean water upon you, and ye shall be clean: from all your filthiness, and from all your idols, will I cleanse you. 26. A new heart also will I give you, and a new spirit will I put within you: and I will take away the stony heart out of your flesh, and I will give you a new heart of flesh. 27. And I will put my spirit within you, and cause you to walk in my statutes, and ye shall keep my judgments, and do them.

The Universal-Key of Spiritual Self-Mastery: Unlocking: the Master within is a book that shall come soon. Chapter 9: is just a roof-draft of the book to come. The bible says that in the book of Jeremiah Chapter 1: verse 5: Before I formed thee in the belly I knew thee; and before thou camest forth out of the womb I sanctified thee, and I ordained thee a prophet unto the nations. The calling and purpose that you possess was given unto you before you came out of your mothers' womb. Out of all those sperm-cells you came forth. My spiritual father Bishop Dr. Delagraentiss always say that we have been here before. God chose you to do something very special for him on this earth. Saul knew that he was a born leader, but he was using his leadership wrong. He said that he persecuted Gods people and that he did this ignorantly. When the Lord begins to give you dreams and visions know that those are angels delivering messages unto you. Many throw their dreams and visions unto the back side; never seeking God for the meaning. Your dreams and visions are seeds. Matthew Chapter 13: verse 19: When any one heareth the word of the kingdom, and understandeth it not, then cometh the wicked one, and catcheth away that which was sown in his heart. This is he which received seed by the way side. Satans job is to steal the word; the seed of God out of your heart. How does satan do this? John Chapter 16: verses 1-3: 1. These things have I spoken unto you, that ye should not be offended. 2. They shall put you out of the synagogues: yea, the time cometh, that whosoever killeth you will think that he doeth God service. 3. And these things will they do unto you, because they have not known the father, nor me.

Key point # 30:

When your prayers are being manifested many shall become very offended. A spiritual shaking begins the happen. Betrayal, rejection will take place because God is doing a separation especially concerning the prophets and seers of God; they know by experience that they must remain secretive and anonymous because of the blood thirsty jezebels. The signs of prayer being manifested is betrayal, and rejection. John Chapter 16: verses 13-15: 13. Howbeit when he, the spirit of truth, is come, he will guide you into all truth: for he shall not speak of himself; but whatsoever he shall hear, that shall he speak: and he will shew you things to come. 14. He shall glorify me: for he shall receive of mine, and shall shew it unto you. 15. All things that the father hath are mine: therefore said I, that he shall take of mine, and shall shew it unto you. As you pray in secret God will reveal unto you the strategy, and onslaught of the devil. The psychology of manifested prayer is in verses 13-15: So when these things happen unto you and all around you know that God separates you from those who are pretending to have your best interest in mind.

Time-travel is real and many take it as a joke, even scientists say that we are limited with our minds. This is because of the fall of man in the garden of Eden. When Adam ate the forbidden fruit and sinned. He never repented of his sin, but Christ said that in John Chapter 16: verse 13: Howbeit when he, the spirit of truth, is come, he will guide you into all truth: for he shall not speak of himself; but whatsoever he shall hear, that shall he speak: and he will shew you things to come. These angels are known as the spirit of Truth. The word of means to come from to proceed from a location. That location is space; an area, realm, or dimension. These angels will guide us into all truth. For he shall not speak of himself because these angels are representatives of Christ. They come not to do their own will, but God's will. There are angels who are so powerful that they can destroy the whole earth instantly, but there is a problem.

Key point # 31:
Revelation Chapter 1: verse 20: The mystery of the seven stars which thou sawest in my right hand, and the

seven golden candlesticks. the seven stars are the angels of the seven churches: and the seven candlesticks which thou sawest are the seven churches. 6 of the angels are corrupt because they made a conscious decision to turn on God. It's like the movie called the Prophecy. These are not angels who fell with satan. These are more powerful angels. Satan is only known for his intellect, because he was, and is very persuasive. God called lucifer his anointed cherub. Anointed meaning that he was no ordinary angel, he's an arch- angel. 6 is the number of man. The bible is word-coded and these are some the mysteries that are locked into the scriptures. The other mysteries and secrets of the bible were taken out. Yes God allowed a lot to be taken out of the bible; because if the wrong hands were to find the true secrets and mysteries of the bible the earth would be destroyed sooner than we think. The 7th angel is in hiding for a time and a time again. This angel are not contaminated. The other 6 angels are contaminated, but and if these 6 angels were to find this 7th angel the world would end instantly; but God will not let it be so. All of these angels are intelligent. These are not demons which are the nephalim who are half-angel; half human. These are real angels.

The bible gives us accounts of the fall of satan. Revelation Chapter 12: 1. And there appeared a great wonder in heaven; a woman clothed with the sun and the moon under her feet and upon her head a crown of twelve stars: 2. And she being with child cried, travailing in birth, and pained to be delivered. 3. And there appeared another wonder in heaven; and behold a great red dragon, having seven heads and ten horns, and seven crowns upon his heads. 4. And his tail drew the third part of the stars of heaven, and did cast them to the earth: and the dragon stood before the woman which was ready to be delivered, for to devour her child as soon as it was born. 5. And she brought forth a man child, who was to rule all nations with a rod of iron: and her child was caught up unto God, and to his throne. 6. And the woman fled into the wilderness, where she hath a place prepared of God, that they should feed her there a thousand two hundred and threescore days. 7. And there was war in heaven: Michael and his angels fought against the dragon; and the dragon fought and his angels, 8. And prevailed not; neither was their place found any more in heaven. 9. and the great dragon was cast out, that old serpent, called the devil, and satan, which deceiveth the whole world: he was cast out into the earth, and his angels were cast out with him. 10. And I heard a loud voice saying in heaven, now is come salvation, and strength, and the kingdom of our God, and the power of his Christ: for the accuser of our brethren is cast down, which accused them before our God day and night. 11. And they overcame him by the blood of the lamb, and by the word of their testimony; and they loved not their lives unto the death. 12. Therefore rejoice ye heavens, and ye that dwell in them. woe to the inhabiters of the earth and of the sea! for the devil is come down unto you, having great wrath, because he knoweth that he hath but a short time. 13. And when the dragon saw that he was cast unto the earth, he persecuted the woman which brought forth the man child. 14. And to the woman were given two wings of a great eagle that she might fly into the wilderness, into her place, where she is nourished for a time, and times, and half a time, from the face of the serpent. 15. And the serpent cast out of his mouth water as a flood after the woman, that he might cause her to be carried away of the flood. 16. And the earth helped the woman, and the earth opened her mouth, and swallowed up the flood which the dragon cast out of his mouth. 17. And the dragon was wroth with the woman, and went to make war with the remnant of her seed, which keep the commandments of God, and have the testimony of Jesus Christ. The obscurity of this prophecy, which has been urged against its genuineness, necessarily results from the highly figurative and symbolical language in which it is delivered, and is, in fact, a strong internal proof of its authenticity and divine original. "For it is a part of this prophecy," as sir Isaac Newton justly remarks, "that it should not be understood before the last age of the world; and therefore it makes for the credit of the prophecy that it is not yet understood. The folly of interpreters has been to foretell times and things by this prophecy, as if God designed to make them prophets. By this rashness they have not only exposed themselves, but brought the prophecy also into contempt. The design of God was much otherwise. He gave this, and the prophecies of the old testament, not to gratify men's curiosities by enabling them to foreknow things, but that, after that they were fulfilled, they might be interpreted by the event; and his own providence, not the interpreter's, be then manifested thereby to the world. For the event of things, predicted many ages before, will then be a convincing argument that the world is governed by providence. For, as the few and obscure prophecies concerning Christ's first coming were for setting up the Christian religion, which all nations have since corrupted, so the many and clear prophecies concerning the things to be done at Christ's second coming, are not only for predicting, but also for effecting a recovery and re-establishment of the long-lost truth, and setting up a kingdom wherein dwells righteousness. The event will prove the apocalypse; and this prophecy, thus proved and understood, will open the old prophets; and all together will make known the true religion, and establish it. There is already so much of the prophecy fulfilled, that as many as will take pains in this study may see sufficient instances of God's promise; but then, the signal revolutions predicted by all the holy prophets, will at once both turn men's eyes upon considering the predictions, and plainly interpret them.

Key Point # 32:
Satan has dominion ship in the earth-realm only over those who are not saved, and can have dominion ship over those that God allows him to test. Satan has been

in governments all over the world in human-form numerous times. Satan is a shape-shifter and his only purpose is to kill, steal, and to destroy. The dragon is the rage of satan. When he appears as an angel of light, he's lucuifer meaning light-bearer. He can shift into the devil which means deceiver. She can shift into satan meaning the God of this world, but when Christ comes and take the church from the earth, then satan will possess a clone body perfect for him to rule this earth. Remember the angels were taught by God how to do things that are very advanced. God never revealed everything unto angels. God never revealed his origin unto them. God will never create anything greater than him. For there is no power but that which is of God. Satan and a third of the angel rebelled against God. God didn't take away their gifts, nor tools. Remember as the scripture says that the gifting's and callings of God are without repentance. So when the scripture says in the book of 1 Peter Chapter 5: verse 8: Be sober, be vigilant; because your adversary the devil, as a roaring lion, walketh about, seeking whom he may devour: He's looking for a body to control, especially those who are in leadership, but Satan and his demons can only go so far. That's why when satan creates a perfect body he's going to possess that body, and thus become the anti-Christ. He cannot possess a human body not yet. Only demons, and unclean spirits can possess and oppress a human body. He can shape-shift and change his form into a human being at will, but he can't until the spirit of God is removed from the earth. 1st Corinthians Chapter 13: verse 11: When I was a child, I spake as a child, I understood as a child, I thought as a child: but when I became a man, I put away childish things. The scripture is talking about maturity. I can remember in my teenage years and in my twenties I heard so many people say it's time for me to grow up. It was not me joking around it was my comprehension. A lot of things I could not understand because I am very intelligent; however my comprehension was very bad. But God have chosen the foolish things to confound the wise. I never finished high school. I dropped out of La Marque high school in La Marque Texas because my mom told me too. I thank God that I received my high school diploma at St. Michaels Learning Academy in 2013. In school my mind was always wandering in the things of science, technology, biology, chemistry, physics, and creating things; but no teacher was able to ever reach out to me. I was very quiet and very silent until the 11th grade. If I would have had someone who could understand me to help me I know that my destiny would been even better. I was called a lot of times in school a dreamer, because even though I was very quiet and very silent most of my school years I day-dreamed. I know it was the gifts inside of me. I can draw very well but when I got out of high school i stopped drawing because I felt inside that there was a greater purpose for me than drawing. Galatians Chapter 4: verse 1: Now I say, that the heir, as long as he is a child, differeth nothing from a servant, though he be Lord of all; I know just like

Saul in the book of acts that I was a natural born leader. I just stood out all the time. We all are Lords over the earth even from birth. We either began to walk into mastery-n. victory, authority. Mastery also means to have control over your emotions; to be disciplined in your gifts, talents, abilities, and profession. When I was a child people thought that I was a psychic because I would tell people things before they come, and everything I said came to pass. I even told people numerous times about things in their life and they were amazed, because everything I said was true. The danger and warnings of psychics is that a lot of them are about money. The majority of psychics operate in divination-meaning the foresight to see. They operate under a demonic-spirit.

Key point # 33:
Just because people can tell you about your life doesn't mean that they are from God. For Jesus many shall come in his name saying they are the Christ. Meaning that they will come in a deceptive form of Godliness. Jesus tells us in the book of Matthew Chapter 7: verse 20:Wherefore by their fruits ye shall know them. The word fruit means their works, or ways. They will smile and pretend to have your best interest in mind, but there only motive is self gain. I have seen so many people who said that they are of God, but their deeds were totally opposite. Remember this is not an opportunity for us to slander them, our opportunity is to pray for them that if they are not saved that God would touch

their hearts to confess Jesus Christ as their personal Lord and savior. If they are saved we should pray that God leads them to repent and turn from their wicked way. Remember we shouldn't judge verbally, nor scandalize someone, especially if they are preachers, because the word will judge them for righteousness if they are obedient unto God. The word of God will judge them if they are workers of iniquity. We only judge by discernment, trying the spirit by the spirit of God within us. So when we judge someone verbally and scandalize their names a curse is instantly placed on us because we came against a creation of God. This is a level of mastery that many fail at. even if they are false that is not our job to condemn them. the only judgment that is to be brought is called warning. in the book of Ezekiel Chapter 3: 1. Moreover he said unto me, son of man, eat that thou findest; eat this roll, and go speak unto the house of Israel. 2. So I opened my mouth, and he caused me to eat that roll. 3. And he said unto me, son of man, cause thy belly to eat, and fill thy bowels with this roll that I give thee. then did I eat it; and it was in my mouth as honey for sweetness. 4. And he said unto me, son of man, go, get thee unto the house of Israel, and speak with my words unto them. 5. For thou art not sent to a people of a strange speech and of an hard language, but to the house of Israel; 6. Not too many people of a strange speech and of an hard language, whose words thou canst not understand. surely, had I sent thee to them, they would have hearkened unto thee. 7. But the house of Israel will not hearken unto thee; for they will not hearken unto me: for all the house of Israel are impudent and hardhearted. 8. Behold, I have made thy face strong against their faces, and thy forehead strong against their foreheads. 9. As an adamant harder than flint have I made thy forehead: fear them not, neither be dismayed at their looks, though they be a rebellious house. 10. Moreover he said unto me, son of man, all my words that I shall speak unto thee receive in thine heart, and hear with thine ears. 11. And go, get thee to them of the captivity, unto the children of thy people, and speak unto them, and tell them, thus saith the Lord God; whether they will hear, or whether they will forbear. 12. Then the spirit took me up, and I heard behind me a voice of a great rushing, saying, blessed be the glory of the Lord from his place. 13. I heard also the noise of the wings of the living creatures that touched one another, and the noise of the wheels over against them, and a noise of a great rushing. 14. So the spirit lifted me up, and took me away, and I went in bitterness, in the heat of my spirit; but the hand of the Lord was strong upon me. 15. Then I came to them of the captivity at Terabit, that dwelt by the river of Chebar, and I sat where they sat, and remained there astonished among them seven days. 16. And it came to pass at the end of seven days, that the word of the Lord came unto me, saying, 17. Son of man, I have made thee a watchman unto the house of Israel: therefore hear the word at my mouth, and give them warning from me. 18. When I say unto the wicked, thou shalt surely die; and thou givest him not warning, nor speakest to warn the wicked from his wicked way, to save his life; the same wicked man shall die in his iniquity; but his blood will I require at thine hand. 19. Yet if thou warn the wicked, and he turn not from his wickedness, nor from his wicked way, he shall die in his iniquity; but thou hast delivered thy soul. 20. Again, when a righteous man doth turn from his righteousness, and commit iniquity, and I lay a stumbling block before him, he shall die: because thou hast not given him warning, he shall die in his sin, and his righteousness which he hath done shall not be remembered; but his blood will I require at thine hand. 21. Nevertheless if thou warn the righteous man, that the righteous sin not, and he doth not sin, he shall surely live, because he is warned; also thou hast delivered thy soul. 22. And the hand of the Lord was there upon me; and he said unto me, arise, go forth into the plain, and I will there talk with thee. 23. Then I arose, and went forth into the plain: and, behold, the glory of the Lord stood there, as the glory which I saw by the river of Chebar: and I fell on my face. 24. Then the spirit entered into me, and set me upon my feet, and spake with me, and said unto me, go, shut thyself within thine house. 25. But thou, o son of man, behold, they shall put bands upon thee, and shall bind thee with them, and thou shalt not go out among them: 26. And I will make thy tongue cleave to the roof of thy mouth, that thou shalt be dumb, and shalt not be to them a reprover: for they are a rebellious house. 27. But when I speak with thee, I will open thy mouth, and thou shalt say unto them, thus saith the Lord God; he that heareth, let him hear; and he that forbeareth, let him forbear: for they are a rebellious house. The order of the prophet is to warn the people of their sin before judgment comes. Now we see conclusively the reason why the prophets are casted out of the churches. Now a prophet born from their mother's womb are the eyes, ears, and the mouthpiece of God. They come to bring warning unto the people of God. Prophets operate also in a government-anointing. The prophets are the bi-mental-consultants unto the apostles. The apostles are the builders of the churches; they come to set divine order in and over the house of God. They come to build and make God a habitation. The prophets come to confirm unto the apostle, bishop, or pastor of the house the word of the Lord. The prophets are sent to be joined unto the apostle to cover and to protect them. The apostle therefore can oversee the churches to make sure the sheep of God are ok. The apostle's job is to battle the princes fallen-angels over that land by spiritual-warfare, only the apostle can go up against fallen-angels. The apostle can come against unclean-spirits, demons, and fallen-angels. The apostle can operate in all the gifts of the spirit. Apostles can operate in miracles. They can actually perform miracles, as stated in the book of mark Chapter 16: verses 15-18: the miracles are secret-revelations that God gives the apostle to perform. Remember the apostle can operate as the pastor, prophet, teacher, and evangelist as the Lord leads them to do so.

Key Point # 34:

The mantle of the apostle can only perform miracles. Mark Chapter 16: verses 15-18; but they can only do it, as the Lord tells and leads them to do so. The mantel of the prophet can only perform magic. The word magic may seem like witchcraft, but I'm referring unto multiplication. Signs, wonders, and miracles are all one, but are alike, and also different in characteristics. Each are the same, but are different in anointing's. Many times the evangelist will operate in the anointing of the prophet, which are signs to confirm the word of the Lord. Evangelists can operate in the gifts of healing, and the gifts of faith for the journey at hand. The prophet is under a creative-anointing which is magic. The anointing that they operate in is the word wonder. The apostle is under the highest-anointing which is miracles. The apostle is like the doctor and the prophet is like the nurse to assist as needed. The pastor, teacher, and the evangelist are very important also, but hear me even, as you are reading this that without the apostle, and the prophet the churches will fall. Be very careful about wearing mantles that God never gave you. We can desire anointing's and God will give it unto us; however there's a difference in desiring an anointing, and being born from birth to do something. The scripture clearly says that in the book of Ephesians Chapter 2: verse 20: And are built upon the foundation of the apostles and prophets, Jesus Christ himself being the chief corner stone; The apostles come to build like a c.e.o. They come to lay the foundation. The prophets are come to confirm the word of the Lord to bring warning and judgment. Even though I said that we should not judge, but only by discernment. Yes, the prophets have the right to judge, but it should be the spirit of God within them that leads them to do so. Luke Chapter 11: verse 49: Therefore also said the wisdom of God, I will send them prophets and apostles, and some of them they shall slay and persecute: Fallen-angels job is to attack the apostolic-ministry. A demons job is to take out the prophet. Unclean-spirits job is to confuse the sheep to turn away from the faith. Prophets and Apostles can join together in warfare to come against fallen-angels a.k.a. princes. The scripture says in the book of Matthew Chapter 18: verses 18-20: 18.Verily I say unto you, whatsoever ye shall bind on earth shall be bound in heaven: and whatsoever ye shall loose on earth shall be loosed in heaven. 19. Again I say unto you, that if two of you shall agree on earth as touching anything that they shall ask, it shall be done for them of my father which is in heaven. 20. For where two or three are gathered together in my name, there am I in the midst of them. heaven is the spirit-realm. Even though we know there is an actual heaven, he's talking about the spirit-realm. When the apostle and the prophet come together in spiritual-warfare to pray against the princes a.k.a. fallen-angels to be removed over an area they must fast, as the Lord directs them. These princes are the generals in satans army, and whatsoever ye shall loose on earth meaning your mind if you believe it to be so by faith shall be manifested in the spirit-realm.

Verse 19: says that if two of you shall agree on earth as touching anything that they shall ask, it shall be done. Now any born again believer can come in agreement with someone for things to manifest, but prophets cannot come against princes fallen-angels themselves. This is where the apostle Paul states in the book of 1st Corinthians Chapter 11: verse 30: For this cause many are weak and sickly among you, and many sleep. Many are sick, & weak for trying to bind demonic forces, The scripture is talking about taking actual communion, but there are those who have not discerned the body of the Lord. The reason why there are so many sick and out of order preachers is, because they are doing things out of order. No I'm not saying that they are bad, because we all make mistakes. Madonna the singer said in her video human-nature; it's human-nature. Remember that the flesh will try and take over at times. That's why we see so many preachers sick, and ill because they are taking on warfare that God never equipped them for. Now here's the stipulation in the book of 1st timothy Chapter 3: verse 1: This is a true saying, if a man desire the office of a bishop, he desireth a good work. The bishop is similar unto the apostle. The bishop is more of an in-house pastor. The apostle does more work on the outside of the church. They come to build churches, and businesses for Gods kingdom. The bishop is basically a more experienced pastor, which is an elder. One who walks in the mastery level of a pastor. They have put in a lot of work to do. The apostle comes to oversee the churches that God has placed them over.

They preach from time to time, but the bishop who is just like an apostle stays in the church feeding the flocks of God. The apostle will feed the flock of God, but the apostle has pastors under them to do that. The apostle's mentor, and develops pastors over their churches. The office of the bishop is similar, and also different.

Key point # 35:
1st timothy Chapter 3: verse 1: This is a true saying, if a man desires the office of a bishop, he desireth a good work. You can desire an anointing from God and God will give it unto you. Warning: be very careful about asking God for a mantel that he never originally intended for you, because there's a price to pay with the anointing.

A lot of rejection, hurt, betrayal, and suffering goes along with the anointing, and yes there are times in which something happens and the pastor dies, or can no longer hold that office. And God will raise up someone to take that persons place, but he always has a ram in the bush. Remember that we shouldn't boast, nor glory in gifts, nor anointing's. Your anointing does not come by your gift, your anointing comes unto you by doing something totally opposite of your gift. The reason for this is so that we won't get arrogant, nor prideful, nor boastful in what we have. It's building character in you. So when the people see you they won't see you, but they'll see Christ in you who is the light. Now you can desire any anointing that you desire, but I'm here to tell you it will cost you everything that you have. 1st king's Chapter 19: verses 20-21: 20. And he left the oxen, and ran after Elijah, and said, let me, I pray thee, kiss my father and my mother, and then I will follow thee and he said unto him, go back again: for what have I done to thee? 21. And he returned back from him, and took a yoke of oxen, and slew them, and boiled their flesh with the instruments of the oxen, and gave unto the people, and they did eat. Then he arose, and went after Elijah, and ministered unto him.

Jesus says in the book of mark Chapter 10: verses 28- 31: 28. Then Peter began to say unto him, lo, we have left all, and have followed thee. 29. And Jesus answered and said, verily I say unto you, there is no man that hath left house, or brethren, or sisters, or father, or mother, or wife, or children, or lands, for my sake, and the gospel's, 30. But he shall receive a hundredfold now in this time, houses, and brethren, and sisters, and mothers, and children, and lands, with persecutions; and in the world to come eternal life. 31. But many that are first shall be last; and the last first. There is a price to pay for the anointing because it will cost you everything to do the will of God for your life. People will think you're crazy and that you have lost your mind, but I'm taking to some saved folks how many of you know that it will cost you everything that you got to walk with the Lord? Matthew Chapter 10: verses 34-39: 34. Think not that I am come to send peace on earth: I came not to send peace, but a sword. 35. For I am come to set a man at variance against his father, and the daughter against her mother, and the daughter in law against her mother in law. 36. And a man's foes shall be they of his own household. 37. He that loveth father or mother more than me is not worthy of me: and he that loveth son or daughter more than me is not worthy of me. 38. And he that taketh not his cross, and followeth after me, is not worthy of me. 39. He that findeth his life shall lose it: and he that loseth his life for my sake shall find it. Christ says that he did not come to send forth peace, but he has come to send a sword. The reason why he said that he's come to send a sword is, because there are people in the family that God has chosen to be preachers; and just like Abram who God later changed his name unto Abram had to leave his family. Abraham's family were carnivores. They were idolatrous people. So God chose Abraham out of the tribe to do a special work for him. The family would have contaminated Abraham even the more. So God has to separate you from your family at times so he can deal with you one to one. The family would only bring doubt, unbelief, and discourage unto Abraham. Abraham had a gift of faith. That's why the scripture says that Abraham became the father of faith. God chose Abraham to be so. Abraham had the challenge of hope God against the hope of the world. The hope of the world that he came from verses the hope of God. Abrahams hope was in God. He was not a perfect person but he had faith. Your cross represents your life, and your body. We must daily reject the flesh, reject our will and desires in order to do what God has chosen for us to do. If we try and find our life Christ said that we would lose our lives, because we don't have the answers Christ does. By us losing our lives by following the Lord Jesus Christ know that we shall find it. Mark Chapter 8: verse 36: For what shall it profit a man, if he shall gain the whole world, and lose his own soul? The scripture is saying two things. # 1. Gaining the world by doing our own will can grant us a guaranteed spot in the lake of fire. # 2. Gaining the world can make you crazy, ill, sick, and much more. Matthew Chapter 7: verses 13-14: 13. Enter ye in at the strait gate: for wide is the gate, and broad is the way, that leadeth to destruction, and many there be which go in there at: 14. Because strait is the gate, and narrow is the way, which leadeth unto life, and few there be that find it. I have a group on my websites and I have groups at yahoo called Mastery 6.0: and this group is about Chapter 9. About mastery, in the book which is to come spiritual-self-mastery: unlocking: the master within: will go into greater detail of mastery. This Chapter is just analyzing mastery. But we will go into more detail of mastery in the book to come.

Chapter 9

The Prophet of Dreams: and the Seer: of Visions

The prophet and the seer are similar, but there's a difference in the two. Prophets have more dreams than seers. Seers have more visions than prophets. Prophets do more talking than seers. Seers do less talking than prophets, there's an order. Seers and prophets are prophets. The seer carries a greater-anointing than the prophet. Not every prophet is a seer. If one is called to be a seer he must first be a prophet. There is a waiting period, then a metamorphosis process. Some apostles are seers, or known as a master prophets. I know unto a lot of people this may seem like blasphemy, but pray and the Lord will give you the same thing. I remember the Lord told me in the year 2005 that I am a pope and it threw my theology away. Pope meaning the word apostle. Some bishops don't even go by the name bishop they just go by the title prophet, or seer. Jesus said in the book of John Chapter 13: verse 35: By this shall all men know that ye are my disciples, if ye have love one to another. It is not about titles, it's about your servant hood unto the Lord. Yes there are so many people who are caught up into the glamour and fashion of titles, but titles and names can get you sent to hell. Matthew Chapter 7: verses 21-23: 21. Not everyone that saith unto me, Lord, Lord, shall enter into the kingdom of heaven; but he that doeth the will of my father which is in heaven. 22. Many will say to me in that day, Lord, Lord, have we not prophesied in thy name? And in thy name have cast out devils? And in thy name done many wonderful works? 23. And then will I profess unto them I never knew you: depart from me, ye that work iniquity. Let's examine these verses in scripture very carefully. The words Lord, Lord in verse 21. is saying that these people have the gift of faith. They know how to press their way unto a breakthrough. Remember that the word of God will produce whether you are working for God, or working for the devil. In verse 22: these people use the name of the Lord, they prophesied in his name, they have cast out devil; and they have done many wonderful works. But in verse 23: the Lord tells them depart from me, ye that work iniquity. Sin and iniquity are the same and yet they are different. They both are wrong; sin is when you go against the word of God. At times you can be ignorant of what you did. Iniquity is when you know what you are doing and don't care about the consequences. The bible says in the book of Psalm Chapter 51: verse 5: Behold, I was sharpen in iniquity; and in sin did my mother conceive me. We all have been exposed to sin in our mother's womb. Curses which are bad habits and bad ways have been introduced unto us. These things which we call bad ways and bad habits is a deception of the devil. These are known as curses. We were shaped in iniquity and in sin did our mother conceived us. The nature of mankind changed when Adam sinned in the Garden of Eden, but Christ came and overcame it all for our sakes. The seers which some are apostles and bishops in disguise can see on greater-scales than a prophet. Seers are more observant than prophets, and prophets are very observant as well. So what if a man or woman of God say that they are an evangelist, pastor, teacher, or prophet; but they are really seers? That doesn't mean that they aren't seers. Some just keep the name as evangelist, pastor, teacher, prophet, or apostle. Jesus said we will know them by their fruits. Are they walking in love? What is your motive to do what you do? A seer is a prophet who see-revelation, the word seer, and they can see into the realm of the spirit in large quantities. Prophets and seers can see unclean-spirits, demons, and princes which are fallen-angels. 1st Samuel Chapter 16: verses 1-5: 1.Andthe Lord said unto Samuel, how long wilt thou mourn for Saul, seeing I have rejected him from reigning over Israel? fill thine horn with oil, and go, I will send thee to Jesse the Bethlehemite: for I have provided me a king among his sons. 2. And Samuel said, how can I go? if Saul hear it, he will kill me and the Lord said, take an heifer with thee, and say, I am come to sacrifice to the Lord. 3. And call Jesse to the sacrifice, and I will shew thee what thou shalt do: and thou shalt anoint unto me him whom I name unto thee. 4. And Samuel did that which the Lord spake, and came to Bethlehem and the elders of the town trembled at his coming, and said, comest thou peaceably? 5. And he said, peaceably am come to sacrifice unto the Lord: sanctify yourselves, and come with me to the sacrifice and he sanctified Jesse and his sons, and called them to the sacrifice. Prophets and seers carry a lot of weight as we see in these scriptures. The prophet Samuel comes into the city. They are known to bring warning and judgment unto the nations. The people were trembling at his coming. A lot of prophets and seers are in hiding under the name psychic, because of the onslaught of the people in the church. The church are the ones who should understand the prophetic ministry. They are the main ones who are beheading the voice of the prophet, and this is why we see a lot of confused prophets; because of the persecution that comes with that office. Many of them have turned from their faith and have went into hiding. Kings and governments sought the legal advice of the prophets and they sought council from the voice of God. The office of the prophet has been attacked over and over again. I am a witness unto the persecution. The prophets come to declare the word of the Lord unto the nations. That's why satan has set up his false prophets in the majority of the churches; and that is why we have so much confusion in the churches when it comes to prophets. No one should come before the prophet empty handed. Scripture says in the book of Matthew Chapter 10: verses 40-41: He that receiveth you receiveth me, and he that receiveth me receiveth him that sent me. 41. He that receiveth a prophet in the name of a prophet shall receive a prophet's reward; and he that receiveth a righteous man in the name of a righteous man shall receive a righteous man's reward. You rob God when you do not bless the prophet. As I stated before that prophets operate in a creative-anointing. They have the uncanny-supernatural ability to bring increase. 1st kings Chapter 17: verses 8-24: 8. And the word of the Lord came unto him, saying, and 9. Arise, get thee to Zarephath, which belongeth to Zidon, and dwell there: behold, I have commanded a widow woman there to sustain thee. 10. So he arose and went to Zarephath. And when he came to the gate of the city, behold, the widow woman was there gathering of sticks: and he called to her, and said, fetch me, I pray thee, a little water in a vessel that I may drink. 11.And as she was going to fetch it, he called to her, and said, bring me, I pray thee, a morsel of bread in thine hand. 12. And she said, as the Lord thy God liveth, I have not a cake, but an handful of meal in a barrel, and a little oil in a cruse: and, behold, I am gathering two sticks, that I may go in and dress it for me and my son, that we may eat it, and die. 13. And Elijah said unto her, fear not; go and do as thou hast said: but make me thereof a little cake first, and bring it unto me, and after make for thee and for thy son. 14.

For thus saith the Lord God of Israel, the barrel of meal shall not waste, neither shall the cruse of oil fail, until the day that the Lord sendeth rain upon the earth. 15. And she went and did according to the saying of Elijah: and she, and he, and her house, did eat many days. 16. And the barrel of meal wasted not, neither did the cruse of oil fail, according to the word of the Lord, which he spake by Elijah. 17. And it came to pass after these things, that the son of the woman, the mistress of the house, fell sick; and his sickness was so sore, that there was no breath left in him. 18. And she said unto Elijah, what have I to do with thee, o thou man of God? art thou come unto me to call my sin to remembrance, and to slay my son? 19. And he said unto her, give me thy son. and he took him out of her bosom, and carried him up into a loft, where he abode, and laid him upon his own bed. 20. And he cried unto the Lord, and said, o Lord my God, hast thou also brought evil upon the widow with whom I sojourn, by slaying her son? 21. And he stretched himself upon the child three times, and cried unto the Lord, and said, o Lord my God, I pray thee, let this child's soul come into him again. 22. And the Lord heard the voice of Elijah; and the soul of the child came into him again, and he revived. 23. And Elijah took the child, and brought him down out of the chamber into the house, and delivered him unto his mother: and Elijah said, see, thy son liveth. 24. And the woman said to Elijah, now by this I know that thou art a man of God, and that the word of the Lord in thy mouth is truth.

Key point # 36:
The prophet comes to bring increase. It is robbery to not bless the prophet. God sustains people to bless the prophet because people are not giving unto the prophet. Jesus said he that receives a prophet shall receive a prophets-reward and that prophets-reward is the anointing on their life to create life and increase.

The prophet is the spokesman, and the representative of God. God has an order and if a person does not have money or something to give the prophet the prophet is therefore not permitted to give the increase. The prophet had to tell the woman to give him some water in a vessel and a morsel of bread in her hand, and she said that she only has enough for her and her son. And when the woman was obedient unto the prophet the scripture says in 1st kings Chapter 17: verses 15-17: that she obeyed the prophet and they all ate. The barrel of meal wasted not, neither did the cruise of oil fail. The word that's in the prophet's mouth has the power to unlock your destiny.

Prophets and seers operate in streams of the anointing. The prophet speaks and declares the word of the Lord, but the seer joins worlds together. They connect the world of the natural with the spirit to make sense of the chaos in your life. Prophets and seers operate in the dimensions of prophetic-impartation. The prophetic word is for edification, exhortation, and comfort. Edify- means to build up, strengthen, to make more effective. Exhort-means to encourage.

Comfort-means to cheer up. Prophecy is used to counteract condemnation and discouragement. Prophecy operates differently in people. In some prophets who are seers is the realm of the seer. Prophets operate in the realm of the spirit, but seers operate in the realm of the seer. True seers are prophets but not all prophets are seers. The word seer-means a different type of prophet who receives a different type of prophetic-revelation or impartation. When a prophet mainly hears from God, and mainly speaks the word of the Lord know that this is prophetic-revelation. A prophet is mainly literal because they have more dreams than a seer. A seer sees more than a prophet. The prophet operates in the communication dimension receiving downloads from the Lord. The seer operates in more in seeing and receiving downloads from the Lord. 2nd Samuel Chapter 24: verse 11: For when David was up in the morning, the word of the Lord came unto the prophet gad, David's seer, saying, 1st chronicles Chapter 29: verse 29: now the acts of David the king, first and last, behold, they are written in the book of Samuel the seer, and in the book of Nathan the prophet, and in the book of Gad the seer, Gad was a seer and Nathan was a prophet. A seer is a prophet but operates in the highest form of the prophetic-impartation. There are streams of the prophetic coming unto Gods people like never before. Mighty streams that shall at times manifest as cloven tongues of fire that shall baptize the saints of God afresh. Acts Chapter 3: verse 19: Repent ye therefore, and be converted, that your sins may be blotted out, when the times of refreshing shall come from the presence of the Lord; Ignition is being in effect like never before. The glory of God shall be revealed in these 7 years 2013 unto 2020 in multiple-streams of Gods power. People in governments, and authority-figures shall see the glory of God on Gods people. and they shall run unto them. Isaiah Chapter 55: verses 1-5: 1. Ho, every one that thirsteth, come ye to the waters, and he that hath no money; come ye, buy, and eat; yea, come, buy wine and milk without money and without price. 2. Wherefore do ye spend money for that which is not bread? And your labour for that which satisfieth not? hearken diligently unto me, and eat ye that which is good, and let your soul delight itself in fatness. 3. Incline your ear, and come unto me: hear, and your soul shall live; and I will make an everlasting covenant with you, even the sure mercies of David. 4. Behold, I have given him for a witness to the people, a leader and commander to the people. 5. Behold, thou shalt call a nation that thou knows not, and nations that knew not thee shall run unto thee because of the Lord thy God, and for the holy one of Israel; for he hath glorified thee. People all over the world in the year 2013 unto the year 2020 shall see the glory of the Lord upon Gods people; and shall come running unto them in the masses. Gods glory flowing in mighty streams like never before shall draw the nations of the world unto the children of light. They shall want to hear about this Jesus that we serve.

Key point # 37:

Ezekiel Chapter 37:5. Thus saith the Lord God unto these bones; behold, I will cause breath to enter into you, and ye shall live: I hear the word of the Lord saying that I am restoring, and am raising up my servants Bishop Carlton Pearson, my servant Bishop Eddie Long, my servant Prophetess Juanita Bynum, my servant Pastor Paula White. Ezekiel 37: 11. Then he said unto me, Son of man, these bones are the whole house of Israel: behold, they say, our bones are dried, and our hope is lost: we are cut off for our parts.

Job Chapter 42: 10: And the Lord turned the captivity of job, when he prayed for his friends: also the Lord gave job twice as much as he had before. These had been under a job test. God is giving his servants double for their trouble. revelation Chapter 2: 17: He that hath an ear, let him hear what the spirit saith unto the churches; to him that overcometh will I give to eat of the hidden manna, and will give him a white stone, and in the stone a new name written, which no man knoweth saving he that receiveth it.

There are seers who mainly operate in the realm of dreams and visions. Seers can operate in the language of dreams depending on their realm of impartation. Although I said that prophets mainly operate in the language of dream. Your seers who are prophets can also operate in the anointing to interprete dreams and visions also. All prophets can operate in dreams and visions depending on their anointing's. You will know the difference of the prophet and the seer who are prophets. Although prophets and seers are similar they also are different too. Prophets and seers will not always have a large crowds. For many are called but few are chosen. Remember that there is an order. Prophets and seers can also work together. While the prophet can see dreams know that the seers not only have dreams, but they mainly are going to see visions. Dreams and visions are angels. They are divine messengers of God. That's why we must be very careful who we entertain because God makes himself known unto the prophets(seers): in a vision, and he speaks to them in a dream. The highest anointing in the prophetic is the seer-anointing. The seer-anointing can also be known, as a master prophet. God has chosen them to have this grace on their lives for the task that he has given them. Prophets are going to do more talking and seers less talking. Prophets will have more dreams than the seer and seers will have more visions than the prophets. The prophets which are also seers are not going to have a large crowd all the time, because many will not understand the mysteries of God. Dreams and visions are divine tools use to make people aware of God. To make people aware of the realm of the spirit, known as the spirit-realm. There are those who are born prophets from their mother's womb who can desire the seer-anointing, but there is a very great price to pay. Prophets are very misunderstood and many will label the prophets and seers bi-polar, schizophrenia, anti-social because many people do not understand the prophetic-order. Prophets and seers are prayer-warriors. The prophet goes into the realm of intercessions interceding for the saints of God. The seers go into the realm of warfare to battle the fallen-angels head on in the name of Jesus. Prophets go into the realm of the spirit to battle and war against demons. Even though the prophetic ministry is still a mystery in these last days God is causing his people to understand the ministry of the prophets. Many are rejected and cast out of the church, because leaders, and clergymen do not understand that these are divine-vessels of God to bring forth divine change. If you remember in the movie X-men part 1 when rogue was in the bar with wolverine she displays the characteristics and actions of a prophet. She was mysterious and misunderstood even her parents could not understand her. John Chapter 10: verses 12-13: 12. But he that is a hireling, and not the shepherd, whose own the sheep are not, seeth the wolf coming, and leaveth the sheep, and fleeth: and the wolf catcheth them, and scattereth the sheep. 13. The hireling fleet, because he is a hireling, and careth not for the sheep. I have been under hirelings who I did not recognize at the time because I was a babe in the things of God. God protected me and he transferred the anointing from these leaders and gave it unto me and others.

Key point # 38:
Just like Bishop Carlton Pearson, Prophetess Juanita Bynum, Bishop Eddie l. Long, Pastor Paula White and so many others who were violently attacked by the body

of Christ have learned to build on their own because of their established relationship with God. Matthew Chapter 23: verse 34: Wherefore, behold, I send unto you prophets, and wise men, and scribes: and some of them ye shall kill and crucify; and some of them shall ye scourge in your synagogues, and persecute them from city to city: Storms, hurricanes, tornadoes, earthquakes, and much more happened on the earth because of the violent opposition that came against the saints of God. Warning unto the body of Christ when you come against a man or woman of God, especially a preacher; damnation, and swift destruction will come unto you. Matthew Chapter 18: verses 6-7: 6. But whoso shall offend one of these little ones which believe in me, it were better for him that a millstone were hanged about his neck, and that he were drowned in the depth of the sea. 7. Woe unto the world because of offences! for it must needs be that offences come; but woe to that man by whom the offence cometh! We are suppose to judge by discernment, and then seek the Lord in prayer concerning Gods people. We are not to condemn, nor judge Gods people by condemnation. Because there are so many false-prophets, and mockers in the body of Christ many in the churches fall for the bait and the deception of satan. There are so many churches that are packed with people who are not saved. Bishop T.D. Jakes did a sermon-series on still not saved and one of the main purposes of why people come to church is because it's like a club; a.k.a. as social- gathering. They have made the church into a cult, and that's why we still have people in the churches that are still not saved who confess Jesus Christ, as their Lord and savior but they just spoke words but did not truly mean it in their hearts. Therefore demon-spirit enters into these people and therefore they become puppets of the devil to try and hinder the move of God. They are assigned by satan to attack the pastor and to scatter the sheep of God from serving in their local churches. This is why we see so many pastors retiring and falling dead, because of the witchcraft that has been secretly planted in the churches. Revelation Chapter 3: verse 18: I counsel thee to buy of me gold tried in the fire, that thou mayest be rich; and white raiment, that thou mayest be clothed, and that the shame of thy nakedness do not appear; and anoint thine eyes with eyesalve, that thou mayest see. The nakedness of Gods people who are the saints should not be exposed to no one. Social media networks love to expose and show the world the nakedness of the church. The world loves gossip and so does the religious secta. We as Christian followers of the Lord Jesus Christ are supposed to pray for one another. Ephesians Chapter 6: verse 18: Praying always with all prayer and supplication in the Spirit, and watching thereunto with all perseverance and supplication for all saints; The problem is that we have saints of God praying for the body of Christ, but we hardly have people praying for the saints of God in the spirit. In the old days the saints of God would stay at the churches for days until a breakthrough came forth. Now we have I dream of Jeannie prayers for instant manifestation.

Everything that looks good is not good. But I hear the word of the Lord saying that he has a remnant in the back parts of the desert hidden that I am about to raise up saith the Lord. Saints that I am about to bring to the forefront to declare the presence of the Lord. There is a great evil that is on the rise that many shall see and behold. Vampires, werewolves, fairies, magicians, wizards and much more are manifesting upon the scene. This is the demonic in operation which is a great evil is here in the earth. These come with signs and lying wonders, these are people who are consulting the dead, those who are using blood sacrifice as a mean to gain power. Let me tell you that unclean-spirits are exercised spirit in those that have died. **W**arning some of these exercised spirits are good and some of them are bad. We see these spirits everyday and they can shape-shift and be in human-form for only a limited time. The limited-time can be for 10 years, 5 years, 1 year, 8 months, 2 months, unto a matter of weeks to days. These are familiar-spirits that are sent from the devil to deceive the lost, and they are sent into the churches to deceive even the very elect. Remember if you are born again, baptized, and filled with the Holy- Ghost know that a spirit can no longer enter into you; however demons and unclean spirits can oppress you. Here's an example if you remember the movie Superman 3 movie, there was a scene with superman and Annette O'toole in which she went to answer the phone and a few seconds later superman stated feeling funny, this is a sign of demonic-influence. A man or woman of God with a cloud of darkness all over them and this is where prophets of God can become prophetic-witches in disguise. Christ said that even the very elect would be deceived. There are millions of people even in the church who are worshipping satan. They are brainwashed into believing that Jesus is not the way unto God. So these people are drawn into occults by demonic-influence thinking that these secret-societies are of God, and they look at the dollar-bill as we God love money. So these people have to sacrifice a love one in their family in order to be apart of these secret-societies. When you kill someone, or have someone killed a curse is therefore placed on you unless you repent. These blood sacrifices are satanic-rituals to summons and to worship the devil and therefore by these people giving a blood sacrifice a demon enters their soul and takes control. Demons are tormentors. Demons as I said many times are the offspring of fallen-angels and humans. People can take the form of cat-like creatures the familiar if they are influenced by the demoniacs.

Key point # 39:
In the group that I have called the Rise of Apocalypse when the Egyptians captured and oppressed the Hebrews the Egyptians made one of the biggest mistakes that they could have ever made when they capture the Hebrews they; therefore set themselves up for destruction. God had cheribums and seraphims disguised as humans. And these angels were to watch over and to protect the Hebrews, as the Hebrews built

the kingdom of the pharaohs. The Hebrews taught the Egyptians the word of God therefore the blood was off of the Hebrews hand and the blood was on the Egyptians. The Egyptians learned how to build like master-architects. At the same time fallen-angels and demons influenced the Egyptians into serving other Gods. Prime example is the cat, the eagle, the sun-God and much more. Remember in the book of Exodus Chapter 20: verse 3: Thou shalt have no other Gods before me. So it was not that the Egyptians were so wise, smart, and intelligent they learned how to do many things by learning from the Hebrews. The pharaohs and the Egyptians changed many of the things of God that were taught unto them by the Hebrews. The fallen-angels had sex with the Egyptians and therefore the Egyptians produced giants like in the book of Genesis Chapter 6: verses 1-8: When the sons: of God: saw the daughters: of men: and had sex with these women and these women produced evil, wicked, and satanic- giants; which is known as the nephalim. And because the Egyptians knew the truth about God and his word they were therefore under the judgment. God was patient then he destroyed the pharaohs and all of Egypt because they served other God. Gods plan was for angels to have sex with humans to produce super-giants, but God did not want the fallen-angels to have sex with humans; because they went against the will of God. So here we come with the rise of Apocalypse: this angel was given a very special gift of time. This angel is going to come from another time-zone when

Christ takes the church from the earth. Remember all the fallen- angels are under satan ruler-ship, even the demons, and unclean-spirits, and the other angels like the death angel is more powerful than satan. Satan has been given grace by God because to rule in the earth because of Adams disobedience. Satan is the God of this world and all the angels good and bad know this until the end.

A lot is found in the Egyptian history about life. A lot of the information was destroyed, and is here in the earth. Many of these documents are hidden, but what's in darkness shall be manifested in the light. Apocalypse is here on the earth and has been here on the earth for centuries. Multitudes of people have seen a lot of movies and look at the movies, as relaxing but in actuality many of the movies that you see are coded. There is a lot of truth in movies but must be discerned. Apocalypse has a healing-chamber like the chamber that you saw in the movie Stargate. Remember that God taught the angels a lot of things; however God never revealed unto the angels about his origin. There is a lot that God never told the angels. So when satan and his angels rebelled against God; he never stripped the angels of their gifts, nor knowledge for the giftings and callings of God are without repentance. There were also angels who fell before satan and were not cast unto other planets. These planets are in space in which we called outer-space. Outer-space is known, as beyond the sphere of the earth. Now the angels who fell with satan were enslaved to serve satan until the end in which Christ would cast them into the lake of fire. Revelation Chapter 19: verse 20: And the beast was taken, and with him the false prophet that wrought miracles before him, with which he deceived them that had received the mark of the beast, and them that worshipped his image, these both were cast alive into a lake of fire burning with brimstone. Satan, and the false prophet were cast into a lake of fire burning with brimstone. Satan is known as the beast. The beast is also referred unto a corrupt economical system. What makes satan the beast because is the multitudes of fallen-angels with him. The multitudes can also be referred to the word train (Isaiah 6:1): which mean abundance. A 3rd of the angels were cast out of heaven with him. When satan and his angels join together there will be great chaos like the chaos when Hitler was in power. Now there are angels that are reserved in everlasting chains. Jude verse 6: And the angels which kept not their first estate, but left their own habitation, he hath reserved in everlasting chains under darkness unto the judgment of the great day. If you examine the solar-system and the star-constellation you will see billions of planets. There were assigned angels to govern the planets. The earth does not belong to Michael, Gabriel, nor unto the other Holy Angels. The earth was assigned and given unto man-kind. The earth was assigned and given unto Lucifer and each angel was given a planet. Why do you think God cast lucifer down unto the earth, because lucifer was to govern the earth. That's why he knew so much about the earth. He knows what could destroy the earth. That's why angels must be invited by those who are born again believers in the Lord Jesus Christ. Satan takes many forms, and likes to take the form of a man and sometimes the form of a woman. When satan fell he and his angels were cast unto the earth. The angels who fell with him were stripped of their government over the planets that they were assigned unto which is one planet (Earth). That's why the fallen-angels are slaves unto the devil because his territory is the earth. You see when God gives you something it's yours'. He was supposed to lead the people, & the angels unto God by worship, but instead he rebelled against God in his heart; as found in the book of Ezekiel Chapter 28, and in the book of Isaiah Chapter 14. Now the book of Revelation Chapter 12: The great dragon is not satan alone. This is satan and the fallen angels as one. This was their train meaning multitudes. The dragon represents the wrath of Satan. The wrath of Satan is the judgment of God that came upon him because of his defiance. He is described as the dragon because he is still an arch-angel of God. The dragon is also a beast mentality. He belongs to God without the anointing this arch- angel Satan is beyond reprobate. Satan is a reprobate angel who rebelled against God.

Key point # 40:
There are many angels who are more powerful than satan, the only reason the fallen-angels and holy angels have not taken out satan is because the earth

is his domain. The holy bible is a combination of holy documents that remained after Constantine and others destroyed all of the other books, except for documents that were hidden satan and his angels did not want mankind to know about the Holy books of God. That's why Christ says in the book of John Chapter 16: verse 13: Howbeit when he, the Spirit of truth, is come, he will guide you into all truth: for he shall not speak of himself; but whatsoever he shall hear, that shall he speak: and he will shew you things to come. The Holy angels of God come to guide us into all truth, not unto facts, but unto truth which is the universal question of why? 1st Peter Chapter 5: verse 8: Be sober, be vigilant; because your adversary the devil, as a roaring lion, walketh about, seeking whom he may devour: satan walketh about as a roaring lion, which means demons which are the nephalim-spirit, the offspring of fallen-angels walketh about like a lion. It's like the movie predator. Satan cannot be everywhere at the same time. So the devils soldiers who are also fallen-angels, demons, and unclean-spirit are set up exactly like a military. They are like birds on a power line. When you pray and go forth into the things of God they are immediately launched to steal, kill, and to destroy you. That's why the 3rd level of tongues when the Holy Ghost prays and intercedes on your behalf confuses the demonic-order, and confuses the demonic-world. Whenever you are praying in the 3rd level of tongues you bring fear unto satan and his army.

Now back unto the prophets and the seers. If you remember the movie X-men part one If you examine Gene Grey she is like the prophet and Professor Xavier is like the seer who is a more advanced prophet. The prophets can see into the Spirit, speak and declare the word of the Lord. The prophets have a lot on their hands. This is the sign of a real prophet, as I have told you before that a true prophet of God has to give instruction, and warning unto the people, or the people's blood will be on the prophet's hand. In the book of Ezekiel Chapter 3: verse 17-21: 17. Son of man, I have made thee a watchman unto the house of Israel: therefore hear the word at my mouth, and give them warning from me. 18. When I say unto the wicked, thou shalt surely die; and thou givest him not warning, nor speakest to warn the wicked from his wicked way, to save his life; the same wicked man shall die in his iniquity; but his blood will I require at thine hand. 19. Yet if thou warn the wicked, and he turn not from his wickedness, nor from his wicked way, he shall die in his iniquity; but thou hast delivered thy soul. 20. Again, when a righteous man doth turn from his righteousness, and commit iniquity, and I lay a stumbling block before him, he shall die: because thou hast not given him warning, he shall die in his sin, and his righteousness which he hath done shall not be remembered; but his blood will I require at thine hand. 21. Nevertheless if thou warn the righteous man, that the righteous sin not, and he doth not sin, he shall surely live, because he is warned; also thou hast delivered thy soul. These are just some of the signs of a real prophet of God. The seer will operate the same way but in different streams according unto their assignment from God. The prophet will be placed in a position like a shepherd to instruct and to warn the people, but the seer will be sent from God to connect the natural-world with the realm of the spirit to make sense of the chaos in your life. Prophets operate the same way, but the seer will be more instance in their seeing than a prophet. The prophets will leave no stone unturned in your life. Seers will be like the president and your prophets will be like the vice-president. A lot of prophets have gone into hiding because of the onslaught of the religious-systems of the church because many of the leaders and elders do not understand the order of the prophets. The word seer has also changed unto apostle, bishop, elder, and so on; that does not mean that an apostle, bishop, elder, and other preachers are seers. Many of prophets have sold out and went under the name psychic, medium, clairvoyant, and much more and they did this because of the persecution that they have undergone. **W**arning against divination many prophets, and seers work and operate in divination which is the foresight to see by seeking and consulting a familiar-spirit they have put themselves and others great danger. There are unclean-spirit and demons talking to many of Gods prophets. Psychics call these spirit mediums and God gives us clear warning about consulting mediums and familiar-spirits in the book of 1st Samuel Chapter 28: verses 6-20: we see king Saul seeking the Lord in prayer and God did not answer him, nor by dreams so Saul went to the witch of En-dor. Saul consulted a witch and what is a witch is a person who tries and go to God without going through Jesus. a witch is a manipulator. A witch is a rebellious person and the warning for people trying to consult a witch will bring curses upon you. Jesus said in the book of Matthew Chapter 8: verse 22: But Jesus said unto him, follow me; and let the dead bury their dead. Luke Chapter 9: verse 60: Jesus said unto him, let the dead bury their dead: but go thou and preach the kingdom of God. Deuteronomy Chapter 13: verses 1-5: 1. If there arise among you a prophet, or a dreamer of dreams, and giveth thee a sign or a wonder, 2. And the sign or the wonder come to pass, whereof he spake unto thee, saying, let us go after other Gods, which thou hast not known, and let us serve them; 3. Thou shalt not hearken unto the words of that prophet, or that dreamer of dreams: for the Lord your God proveth you, to know whether ye love the Lord your God with all your heart and with all your soul. 4. Ye shall walk after the Lord your God, and fear him, and keep his commandments, and obey his voice, and ye shall serve him, and cleave unto him. 5. And that prophet, or that dreamer of dreams, shall be put to death; because he hath spoken to turn you away from the Lord your God, which brought you out of the land of Egypt, and redeemed you out of the house of bondage, to thrust thee out of the way which the Lord thy God commanded thee to walk in. So shalt thou put the evil away from the midst of thee. I have groups that I did and you can look them up online called Dreamer: of Dreams and I used Jack Nicholas from the movie batman part one in which Jack Nicholas played the character of the joker; and I used the joker as a false-prophet, a wolf in sheep-clothing . This is what happened unto king-Saul so when people say that they don't want to go to church because there are hypocrites there, then they don't understand the scripture in verse 3: that says for the Lord your God proveth you, to know whether ye love the Lord your God with all your heart and with all your soul. It is not to prove it unto God. What he's saying is that it's for your sake. In the future you will know the spirit and you will know how this spirit operates, as you seek the Lord in prayer. Apostle Jonas-Clark talks about this type of spirit on his website. How prophets are becoming prophetic-witches in disguise, a.k.a. pimps in the churches. So God allows these spirits to come into his house because he desire that non perish. Not all come to repentance, he still gives them a chance to repent. God will allow the wolves to enter the churches because it's spiritual-training for your destiny. These so called prophets which are dreamers of dreams can operate just like a real prophet of God, but here's the difference. This jezebel-spirit spirit can show you a sign or a wonder and these signs and wonders can come to pass that's why Jesus said in the book of Matthew Chapter 24: verses 4-5: 4. And Jesus answered and said unto them, Take heed that no man deceive you. 5.For many shall come in my name, saying, I am Christ; and shall deceive many. Many shall be deceived by the signs and wonders of these false- prophets. This spirit will not just operate in preachers, but this spirit is operating in every profession; and this spirits job is to get you to serve other Gods. The dreamer of dreams is a magician, wizard, clairvoyant, soothsayer, tarot-card reader, and much more. When you careful read and observe the jezebel-spirit in the book of Revelation Chapter 2: verses 19-25: this spirit observes your works, charity, service, faith, and your patience because this jezebel-spirit knows that manifestation is about to happen so it tries to hi-jack your manifestation from coming by getting you to turn from God, and getting you to serve other Gods. See when you turn your focus, attention and direction from God you therefore leave his protection. The jezebel spirit comes to steal your focus, and your attention. This spirit also comes to destroy your patience. It comes to kill your dreams from manifesting to try to get you into a fantasy state of mind. That's why we must be careful because the devil has imitations also. Just because someone can show you signs and wonders and these signs and wonders come to pass does not mean that they are of God. Let us examine 2nd Thessalonians Chapter 2: verses 7-12: 7. For the mystery of iniquity doth already work: only he who now letteth will let, until he be taken out of the way. 8. And then shall that Wicked be revealed, whom the Lord shall consume with the spirit of his mouth, and shall destroy with the brightness of his coming: 9. Even him, whose coming is after the working of satan with all power and signs and lying wonders, 10. And with all deceivableness of unrighteousness in them that perish; because they received not the love of the truth, that they might be saved. 11. And for this cause God shall send them strong delusion, that they should believe a lie: 12. That they all might be damned who believed not the truth, but had pleasure in unrighteousness. The mystery of iniquity, which is the secret of the devil and how he operates has been in operation from when he was in heaven. He has disguised himself as other gods, and many other gods to deceive nations and cultures from the beginning of time. Who is he that letteth? The one who allows the devil to operate is God and I know this may blow a lot of people away; but this is true until he be taken out of the way even though the scripture uses the word he in verse 7: satan shall have a male body that is a clone to possess when Christ takes the church away from the earth the wicked shall be revealed by the mouth of his servants. Matthew Chapter 10: verse 27: What I tell you in darkness, that speak ye in light: and what ye hear in the ear, that preach ye upon the housetops. The Lord shall consume with the spirit of his mouth by his servants. You have those who are working for the devil consciously, and those who are working for the devil and who knew what they are doing is wrong. They come with signs and lying wonders to get you to turn from God to serve idols to serve other gods. These lying wonders will look like miracles of God, but they are counterfeit. The one who is coming when Christ comes to get the church from the earth is satan, and satan shall have a cloned-body to possess. In these false-prophets signs and false-miracles (lying wonders), is deception. They are deceived because of their unlawful acts. These are Scribes, Pharisees, and Sadducees, and they perish because they have their conscious seared with a hot-iron which means that they have a strong-will and are under great deception. This is the judgment of God unless they repent, because they receive not the love of the truth that they might be saved. These people are so deceived that they can't even recognize, nor understand salvation. A lot of these people operate in old-testament laws and principles which is the law. God shall send them strong-delusion that they should believe a lie, strong-delusions of worldly-gain, strong delusions of false-prophets, even greater than them in disguise that they cannot discern that they are false. Matthew Chapter 24: verses 11-12. 11. And many false prophets shall rise, and shall deceive many. 12. And because iniquity shall abound, the love of many shall wax cold. Matthew Chapter 24: verses 23-28: 23. Then if any man shall say unto you, lo, here is Christ, or there; believe it not. 24. For there shall arise false Christ's, and false prophets, and shall shew great signs and wonders; insomuch that, if it were possible, they shall deceive the very elect. 25. Behold, I have told you before. 26. Wherefore if they shall say unto you, behold, he is in the desert; go not forth: behold, he is in the secret chambers; believe it not. 27. For as the lightning cometh out of the east, and shineth even unto the west; so shall also the coming of the son of man be. 28. For wheresoever the carcass is, there will the eagles be gathered together. The love of many shall wax cold meaning that even those who are saved and were filled with the Holy Spirit are just saved. They have vexed, and have grieved the Holy Spirit by following others gods. They are operating in their carnality instead of them letting God lead them. They lead themselves unto destruction and do not see it. There shall arise false-Christs and false-prophets. Holograms and many people shall be so bound with demons and they shall truly believe in their hearts that they are Jesus Christ the son of God. Many shall follow these false-Christ and they all shall fall into destruction. False-prophets not just people in every profession, but preachers, and people proclaiming to be true prophets of God. These are known, as wolves hirelings in sheep-clothing. The number one sign to see if someone is a false-Christ, false-prophet which are hireling's wolves in sheep's-clothing is that they will run when trouble comes. They can discern disaster before and when it comes at times. They will pretend to have your back, but when they sense danger they will leave for good. They will try and find other victims to run game on, even the very elect will be deceived, but not all. The number one sign to know if someone is false is seek the spirit of God in which Christ says in the book of John Chapter 16: verse 13: That the spirit of God will guide you into all truth the world truth is called fact but Gods truth is all truth the whole package. Many people who shall be under the deception of satan will try and tell the people of God that he's in the desert, or in the secret-chambers.

Warning: this is a trap from the enemy. If you are saved, baptized, and filled with the Holy-Ghost then Christ is in you. You should have a shepherd (pastor): to cover you. Many so called born again believers go and run from state to state, from city to city to see their favorite preacher. They have made the man, or woman of God their God, and they have put God to the backside. It's ok to visit and go to conferences, but make sure that you are led by the Lord before going. There are many preachers who are not called by God. Many of them only took the title of a preacher for the money. These are hireling's false-prophets, wolves in sheep's-clothing. The bible tells us in the book of 1st John Chapter 4: verse 1: Beloved, believe not every spirit, but try the spirits whether they are of God: because many false prophets are gone out into the world. Scripture is letting us know that we must try the spirit. Remember that our pastors told us to watch, listen, look and to observe everyone and everything at all times. We are to do this so that we may know what to pray for. We are to watch also in the Spirit at all times for all saints for all people. When we try the spirit to know if they are of God, or the devil; we are to be quiet and listen unto what is being said by the other person so the Lord can deal with us. By listening to the spirit of God we will know who they are if they are real, or false. Many preachers only come into the churches to build only for financial-gain. These are hirelings and they do not care for the things of God; nor do they care for Gods people. Over 89% of Christians have been under false-shepherds, that's why the majority of any Christian friends, or associates that you talk too will let you know about the order of the shepherd and pastor that they have been under. That does not mean for you to stop going to church, but even I myself have been greatly hurt time after time in the churches, but we must always remember hurt people hurt people. Our job as born again Holy Ghost filled Christians is to pray for everyone and mainly keep the shepherds of the house in prayer at all times. There are demonic-forces working on the outside. When God prophesies unto you he's confirming what he has already said.

There are 12 operations of prophetic-impartation:

1. Prophetic-Equippers-prophet-teacher. This is the grace to equip others like a teachers which is commonly known as a theologian. Prophetic-Equippers can equip people by mentorship hands on one on one, or by the people listening unto them and watching their lifestyles.

2: Prophetic-Intercessors-people under the anointing of God who takes the burden of the people from God, whether it be individuals, cities, communities, or nations.

3: Prophetic-Counselors-people with the prophetic anointing like a shepherd, or pastor that operates under a healing-anointing. Luke Chapter 4: verses 18-19: 18. The spirit of the Lord is upon me, because he hath anointed me to preach the gospel to the poor; he hath sent me to heal the brokenhearted, to preach deliverance to the captives, and recovering

of sight to the blind, to set at liberty them that are bruised, 19. To preach the acceptable year of the Lord. These types of people can quickly discern the hurts, and pains that others are going through. They will have a heart like a pastor. These types of people have the gift of compassion to love the unlovable. This is the grace of God upon their lives to minister unto the needs of Gods people.

\# 4: Spirit-Bearers-these are people who can operate in the geographics, and timing of the Spirit. These people attract the Spirit of God, as they bathe in his presence. These people can see into the realm of the spirit. They attract Gods presence for the atmosphere they are in. These people as in the book of Colossians Chapter 1: verse 16: can see and sense heaven, earth, the visible, the invisible, thrones, dominions, principalities, powers, angels, demons, unclean-spirits. They are very sensitive unto the spirit of God.

\# 5: Prophetic-Worship leaders are people who usher in the presence of God by prophetic-worship. They are like David who was a psalmist. These people usher in the presence of God so that the saints of God can draw closer unto the Lord. A lot of the prophetic-worship leaders are very radical and their prophetic-worship is also used as a tool for intercession, praise, worship, and spiritual-warfare. These people tear-down the walls of the devil. They usher in Gods-presence so that the people of God can have super-natural encounters with God.

6: Prophetic-Writers-these people move under a prophetic-anointing. They write prophetic-literature as they are moved by the Holy-Ghost. These people flow like prophets, but their prophetic-impartation is mainly used to write down what the Lord downloads unto them. I have a group called prophetic- literature online with William Shakespeare on the group as my logo. Prophetic-Writers operate more in their writings than just the spoken word of the Lord. Gods uses them to do more inspired writing.

7: The Prophet of Dreams and the Seers of Visions-these prophets operate in the prophetic-anointing, both are similar, and yet both are different. The prophet operates more in the realm of dreams. The seer will operate more in vision, both are prophets. Dream and vision interpretation is an anointing that I flow under a lot. The Lord has given me the ability to interpret people's dreams and visions. As I hear the persons dream or vision I then listen unto the Holy Spirit, and the Holy Spirit tells me what they mean. Dreams and visions must match the bible, and even if they match the bible a person under the discernment-anointing must carefully hear from the Lord for the understanding. This is a tool used to draw people unto the Lord.

8: Prophetic-Government-these are people who operate in the prophetic on a larger-scale to perfect the body of Christ. These are mainly your seers who usually do not prophesy unto people one on one,

but their prophetic-gift is used like in Seerology. Seerology is a group that I have online in which the seer can discern times and seasons. These seers give direction unto the local church, unto governments, unto administrations. A primary example of these seers who operate in prophetic-government is: Prophets the Eyes, Ears, and the Mouthpiece of God:This revelation was given unto me on June 8, 2011: wed: @ 5:29 pm

Prophecy has a science, craft, skill, and technique. There is the discipline, meditation, genesis, alpha, omega, and technology of prophecy.

Universal prophecy- There is the government of prophecy, the law, purpose, and principles of prophecy, history of prophecy- which is the culture of prophecy, the past, present, and the future of prophecy. Compass of prophecy which is the regions, territory, location, area, and atlas of prophecy: The geographical locations of prophetic events, and events to come of the world. The prophetic economics and prophetic wealth empowerment of prophecy: Seasons of prophecy: Seasons to come, prophetic seasons of time, dates, and years. The Major Prophets and you have the Minor Prophets: The sacred art of tongues: 1. tongues is a priestly ministry. 2. tongues is apostolic. 3. stop speaking the worldly, stop cursing. 4. speak as the oracle which is the messenger of God: 5. nationality of; tongues by speaking in different nationality of languages having never learned. 6. tongues speaking to God, the Holy Ghost, which is the Holy Spirit, speaking to God, praying to God on your behalf.

Neophyte-greek: neos-a new convert 2. convert- a new beginner, novice.

Minstrel of the prophet-noun a medieval poet and musician who sang or recited while accompanying himself on a stringed instrument, either as a member of a noble household or as an itinerant troubadour.

2. a musician, singer, or poet. Minstrel of the prophet, instrument of the prophet, prophets are tuned into music, praise and worship like king David. The Psalmist of the prophet: the sacred song, songs, of God, psaltery, tabret, pipe, and harp. One who plays instrument like Prophet Kim Clement:

4 Season 4 angels of the earth:

4 Doors of: opportunities open to Gods people yearly and can open more than that according to your faithfulness, and obedience unto God.

Amos 3: 7: Surely the Lord God will do nothing but he revealeth his secret unto his servants the prophets.

2nd chronicles 20:20 And they rose early in the morning, and went forth into the wilderness of Tekoa:

and as they went forth, Jehoshaphat stood and said, hear me, o Judah, and ye inhabitants of Jerusalem; believe in the Lord your God, so shall ye be established; believe his prophets, so shall ye prosper.

Prophets are known as dreamers because their prophetic-impartation is mainly in dreams. Prophets do more talking than seers. Now your seers are known, as visionaries because of their prophetic-impartation which is mainly in visions. Prophets will have visions but mainly dreams. Seers who are prophets will have dreams but mainly visions. The one who can see and discern in a greater-scale of the prophetic-anointing is the seer. A seer is a prophet who sees revelation can see into the realm of the spirit and in the realm of the seer in larger-scales. When you connect a prophet and a seer together you will have a very unstoppable-force to be reckoned with. While your prophets will bring forth instruction, guidance, warning, and judgment unto the nations. The prophets have a very dangerous job to do as stated in the book of Ezekiel Chapters 2-3. Now the seer can operate like the prophet, because before they became a seer they operated as a prophet, then they were elevated. When you use the word prophet it is talking about the prophet one who is born to be one in their mothers womb, but when you use, or hear the word prophets most likely it's talking about your prophets and seers, even though a seer is a prophet. The seer will operate at the highest-prophetic anointing greater than a prophet. The seer will mainly stand before kings, queens, governments, authorities, to give purpose and direction unto whatever area, location geographically they are assigned unto.

9: Prophetic-Helps-prophets who take care and support the fatherless, orphans, and the widows. James Chapter 1: verse 27: Pure religion and undefiled before God and the Father is this, To visit the fatherless and widows in their affliction, and to keep himself unspotted from the world. These prophets will have unctions from the Lord for the orphans, the fatherless, and the widows. This is the area of anointing in which they operate in. These types of prophets are led into dangerous territories to help those who cannot help themselves. They are extensions of Gods-hand to minister unto the peoples needs. These prophets will work with community-centers, ministries to try and open doors for the less fortunate.

10: Prophetic-Evangelists-these are people who area of ministry is beyond the walls of the church. They are similar unto prophetic-helps, but prophetic-evangelists are led of the spirit to go into communities, streets, neighborhoods, and organizations to minister unto the needs of others. A lot of your evangelist will flow under the prophetic-anointing; this does not mean that they are prophets. God will allow at times the spirit of prophecy to fall on them as their ministering unto others, as a tool to draw people unto the Lord.

They can also desire to be a prophet, but it will not be the same as being called from your mothers-womb to be a prophet. The prophetic-anointing is very vital for evangelist that many will think they are prophets, because the prophetic-anointing is so needed out there in their sphere; area of ministry.

11: Prophetic-Administration-these a people who operate in an administrative-anointing. They have and walk in strategy for administering guidance, and instruction unto those in leadership. The bible gives accounts of people in the bible like Joseph whom pharaoh summoned from the pit unto the palace. Joseph gave pharoah the interpretation of his dreams, and he gave pharoah administrative- instructions to look for a man that is wise and discrete and set him over the land of Egypt. This is a sign of a leader and this is a sign of prophetic-administration. These people walk in great administrative-skills, and walk in great strategies-resolution to any problem.

12: Prophetic-Morality-these people usher in the fruit of the spirit. They mainly are primary examples of the book of Leviticus, which means priesthood, holiness, and access unto God. They will be more like evangelists, but they walk in a high level of holiness. They not only talk the talk, but they live a pure righteous life unto God. These people can be prophetic even though they are not prophets. These are people who do not judge by appearance, but they judge by the heart. Their judgment is discernment and they draw people to

live a holy, consecrated life unto the Lord. Daniel was a type of prophetic- morality in the book of Daniel Chapter 1: verse 8: But Daniel purposed in his heart that he would not defile himself with the portion of the king's meat, nor with the wine which he drank: therefore he requested of the prince of the eunuchs that he might not defile himself. Daniel moved as a seer in the realm of dreams and visions. Usually people who operate in prophetic-morality have a high level of mastery in the things of God, especially their lifestyles.

Prophetic-Confrontation:

Jeremiah Chapter 28: 1: And it came to pass the same year, in the beginning of the reign of Zedekiah king of Judah, in the fourth year, and in the fifth month, that Hannah the son of Azur the prophet, which was of Gibeon, spake unto me in the house of the Lord, in the presence of the priests and of all the people, saying, 2. Thus speaketh the Lord of hosts, the God of Israel, saying, I have broken the yoke of the king of Babylon. 3. Within two full years will I bring again into this place all the vessels of the Lord's house, that Nebuchadnezzar king of Babylon took away from this place, and carried them to Babylon: 4. And I will bring again to this place Jeconiah the son of Jehoiakim king of Judah, with all the captives of Judah, that went into Babylon, saith the Lord: for I will break the yoke of the king of Babylon. 5. Then the prophet Jeremiah said unto the prophet Hannah in the presence of the priests, and in the presence of all the people that stood in the house of the Lord, 6. Even the prophet Jeremiah said, amen: the Lord do so: the Lord perform thy words which thou hast prophesied, to bring again the vessels of the Lord's house, and all that is carried away captive, from Babylon into this place. 7. Nevertheless hear thou now this word that I speak in thine ears, and in the ears of all the people; 8. The prophets that have been before me and before thee of old prophesied both against many countries, and against great kingdoms, of war, and of evil, and of pestilence. 9. the prophet which prophesieth of peace, when the word of the prophet shall come to pass, then shall the prophet be known, that the Lord hath truly sent him. 10. Then Hannah the prophet took the yoke from off the prophet Jeremiah's neck, and brake it. 11. And Hannah spake in the presence of all the people, saying, thus saith the Lord; even so will I break the yoke of Nebuchadnezzar king of Babylon from the neck of all nations within the space of two full years. and the prophet Jeremiah went his way. 12. Then the word of the Lord came unto Jeremiah the prophet, after that Hannah the prophet had broken the yoke from off the neck of the prophet Jeremiah, saying, 13. Go and tell Hannah, saying, thus saith the Lord; thou hast broken the yokes of wood; but thou shalt make for them yokes of iron. 14. For thus saith the Lord of hosts, the God of Israel; I have put a yoke of iron upon the neck of all these nations, that they may serve Nebuchadnezzar king of Babylon; and they shall serve him: and I have given him the beasts of the field also. 15. Then said the prophet Jeremiah unto Hannah the prophet, hear now, Hannah; the Lord hath not sent thee; but thou makest this people to trust in a lie. 16. Therefore thus saith the Lord; behold, I will cast thee from off the face of the earth: this year thou shalt die, because thou hast taught rebellion against the Lord. 17. So Hannah the prophet died the same year in the seventh month. Whenever there is a true prophet of God there will be false prophets on the rise also. When false prophets show up then know of a surely that good is about to manifest on your behalf. The prophet Hannah broke the yoke from off of the prophet jeremiahs neck, but the Lord speaks to Jeremiah and tells him to tell the prophet Hannah that he has broken the yoke of wood, but he shall make for them yokes of iron. Since Hannah was a false prophet and prophesied unto the people Jeremiah tells Hannah amen the Lord do so, and he tells Hannah in the presence of the people, and in the presence of the priests that the prophets of old prophesied against many countries, against kingdoms of war, and against evil and pestilence. Jeremiah told the prophet Hannah that the prophets that prophesy of peace if it's true it will come to pass. The words that the prophets speak will come to pass if they are from God. Jeremiah then tells the prophet Hannah that the Lord did not send him, and that he causes the people to trust in a lie. This type of psychology that Hannah used is known as a lying-wonder. The sign is the word of the Lord, but the wonder is a lie (a lying wonder, a fantasy). Jeremiah tells Hannah that God will cast him from the face of the earth, and tells him that he shall die; because he has taught rebellion against the Lord. Hannah died that same year. False prophet going forth prophesying the Lord said and he didn't say are in danger of eternal damnation like the prophet Hannah. People prophesying out of their own hearts saying God said and he didn't say shall fall out dead, because they used the name of the Lord in vain. The Lord give specific-warnings unto these false-prophets false-shepherds. Ezekiel Chapter 34: verse 2:Son of man, prophesy against the shepherds of Israel, prophesy, and say unto them, thus saith the Lord God unto the shepherds; woe be to the shepherds of Israel that do feed themselves! should not the shepherds feed the flocks? There are many so false-prophets who disguise themselves, as sheep, but in essence these are wolves in sheep's-clothing. They do not care for Gods people. They are only after money. A true-shepherd of God is will not be after money, but will watch for the souls of Gods people. God will take care of his own shepherds. God will move upon the peoples heart to bless the shepherds with money. That does not mean that they are false. So shepherds will not pastor a church, or feed the sheep unless you give them a certain amount are false. Yes the bible does say that the laborer is worthy of his hire. Luke Chapter 10: verse 7: And in the same house remain, eating and drinking such things as they give: for the laborer is worthy of his hire. Go not from house to house. The scripture is not only talking about when you visit someone's house. The scripture is saying in reference to those that the Lord place over a house that he will provide. God will touch the people's heart to give to the house of God, as giving it unto the Lord. God will also touch the people's heart to bless the shepherd and ministers of the house of God. So what if the people in the churches are not giving, then the scripture says in the book of Deuteronomy Chapter 8: verse 18: But thou shalt remember the Lord thy God: for it is he that giveth thee power to get wealth, that he may establish his covenant which he sware unto thy fathers, as it is this day. God will download ideas unto the shepherds to prosper. God will give them businesses to create to generate finances. I have been in a lot of churches where they have shut the doors and would not let anyone leave, because they are a few dollars short. They were a few dollars short to pay their bills, and yes the monies were designed to take care of the churches. The monies were designed to bless the shepherd of the house and the workers, but if the people are not doing their part as giving their tithes, offerings, and their first-fruits known that they are not robbing the church, nor the shepherd, nor the workers of the church, but are robbing God. Malachi Chapter 3: verses 8-12: 8. Will a man rob God? yet ye have robbed me. but ye say, wherein have we robbed thee? in tithes and offerings. 9. Ye are cursed with a curse: for ye have robbed me, even this whole nation. 10. Bring ye all the tithes into the storehouse, that there may be meat in mine house, and prove me now herewith, saith the Lord of hosts, if

I will not open you the windows of heaven, and pour you out a blessing, that there shall not be room enough to receive it. 11. And I will rebuke the devourer for your sakes, and he shall not destroy the fruits of your ground; neither shall your vine cast her fruit before the time in the field, saith the Lord of hosts. 12. And all nations shall call you blessed: for ye shall be a delightsome land, saith the Lord of hosts. Those who do not tithe and give offerings unto God he will curse. In other words God will turn them over unto a reprobate-mind back over unto the devil, and they will be seven times worse than before. You are not giving to a man or woman of God know that you are giving unto the Lord. That what God says that he will rebuke the devourer for your sakes. God promised to open up the windows of heaven and pour you out a blessing to the point that there will not be room enough to receive it. He is talking about abundance. Only a few people have ever given me a tithe, or a offering, and I am grateful because they didn't give it unto me they gave it unto the Lord. I prayed and asked the Lord what he wanted me to do with it. God has already blessed me abundantly, especially in the area of creativity. Ideas just come to me all the time. There are many prophets who are operating under the influence of divination which is the foresight to see. Anytime you have a prophet, or someone who is operating in divination they are not of God. They are connected unto demons which demons know about people lives, especially the past. God is not interested in your past. God is interested in your future.

He speaks to your potential to get you to move forward into your divine-destiny. Watch out for those who always have a word for you. When God uses his prophets to minister the word of the Lord it's not going to be about good things all the time. Prophets come to bring instruction, warning, and judgment if needs be. Prophecy is used for the edifying, exhortation, and for comfort. The main purpose of prophecy is to confirm unto someone what God has already said to give you hope and comfort. Watch out for prophets who are always wanting money for a word. They are not of God. They are prostituting the word of God. These are hireling's wolves in sheeps- clothing. They do not care for Gods people. They only come into the churches and to give a word for financial- gain. They do not care for God's word, nor do they care for Gods people. God is revealing unto his true saints who they are, and how they operate. In the year 2009 I had a revelation from the Lord, then the spirit of God shifted me into tongues, and I translated everything the spirit of God revealed unto me. He told me to tear- down the walls of the devil. It's jezebel and her eunuchs'; workers trying to change the truth of Gods-word. Jezebel is a spirit of defiance to rebel against God. This spirit is so rebellious that it has no respect for leadership. Jezebel releases witchcraft against your mind and emotions. Jezebel loves replacing leadership with her false leadership. Remember that jezebel wants control. When you see someone who wants control all the time know that this is jezebel. There is a difference in wanting respect and wanting control to manipulate others. People you would have never guessed in a lifetime are under jezebels control. So when the Lord had me to read in the year 2009 Jeremiah Chapter 1: verse 10: see, I have this day set thee over the nations and over the kingdoms, to root out, and to pull down, and to destroy, and to throw down, to build, and to plant. When I read this scripture the spirit of God revealed unto me, as I was in tongues how to dismantle jezebel. I said my God, and I went into a very deep trance. The Lord showed me a lot of people who were in the occult under jezebels control. Many people are involved in blood sacrifice, as this is required by jezebel. There were so many people even famous people, politicians, actors, sports-stars, and much more who I saw who were being controlled by the jezebel spirit. All I do know is that an angel took me into the spirit, and revealed unto me how the jezebel spirit operates. After the angel showed me these visions I remember I was on the floor and I was in a deep trance for over 4 hours. That was the longest I had ever been in the spirit. Jezebel and her workers are camouflaged as regular organization all over the world. They are set up to overthrow governments, take people out who will not do as they say. They are set up to oppress countries, cities, states, and communities. We are about to see many signs of the anti-Christ. Remember I said that satan shall possess the body of a clone when Christ takes the church from the earth. A seer-a person who see; observer. a person who prophesies future events; prophet. a person endowed with profound mental and spiritual insight, or knowledge: a wise person, or sage who possesses intuitive powers of divination: as a crystal gazer: or; a psalmist. an inveterate seer: of sights: a clairvoyant, a prophet. Remember seers are prophets, but not every prophet is a seer. Out of the 5-fold ministry we have the apostle, the prophet, pastor, teacher, and the evangelist. In essence when you say seer you are talking about the prophet, but that does not mean they are prophets. The word seer can be used in all the 5-fold. That's why I told you that the apostle, prophet, pastor, teacher, and evangelist can be seers. They may not want to go by that title because the word seer was a word for prophet in the old testament in the book of 1st Samuel Chapter 9: verse 9: seers can go by the name elder, apostle, prophet, pastor, teacher, or evangelist. The main reason they chose to go by these names rather than the seer is because they are not caught up in titles.

Key Point # 41:

Warning there are many who want even talk to you if you don't call them by their clergy name; watch out for this is a sign of a false-prophet. Titles are nothing. It's all about having and walking in the character of Christ. That's why the scripture says in the book of Matthew Chapter 7: verse 20: Wherefore by their fruits ye shall know them. 2nd Corinthians Chapter 11: verses 13-15: 13.For such are false apostles, deceitful workers, transforming themselves into the apostles of Christ. 14. And no marvel; for satan himself is transformed into an angel of light. 15. Therefore it is no great thing if his ministers also be transformed as the ministers of righteousness; whose end shall be according to their works. These false-prophets most likely know the word of God more than you or I. Just because someone can quote scripture, give you a word, or know all about the bible does not mean they are sent from God. You shall know them by their fruit if they are from God. They will humble themselves unto authority. They will walk in love and display the fruit of the Spirit. Watch out for people asking you questions, because this is also a sign that they are not from God.

People can ask you questions, but question after question is a sign that they are false. Questions as for as direction is good. In Chapter 11: we will be going into witchcraft-probing. This is a methodology of a false-prophet someone under the influence of witchcraft. Your prophets operate under a creative-anointing, and so does the seer depending of the level of impartation the prophets will operate in the science and art of visualization. in the dictionary visualization- defined: as; seeing: and feeling: yourself in your own mind; in your imagination: already being a certain way. but we know this is mans definition of visualization. and the visualization that prophets have can be either through dreams and visions. by spiritual-visions, trans- visions, and spiritual-visions. this is known as visionary-revelation. God speak unto us by dreams, visions, and by trances. trances are spiritual-visions, trans-visions, and open-visions. dreams happen a lot of times while you are asleep. visions mainly happen while you are awake. numbers Chapter 12: verse 6: and he said, hear now my words: if there be a prophet among you, I the Lord will make myself known unto him in a vision, and will speak unto him in a dream. dreams can also be given unto people who are not saved, nor are called to be a preacher. Joel Chapter 2: verses 28-29: 28. And it shall come to pass afterward, that I will pour out my spirit upon all flesh; and your sons and your daughters shall prophesy, your old men shall dream dreams, your young men shall see visions: 29. And also upon the servants and upon the handmaids in those days will I pour out my spirit. acts Chapter 2: verses 17-18: 17. And it shall come to pass in the last days, saith God, I will pour out of my spirit upon all flesh: and your sons and your daughters shall prophesy, and your young men shall see visions, and your old men shall dream dreams: 18. And on my servants and on my handmaidens I will pour out in those days of my spirit; and they shall prophesy: The anointing that prophets operate under is in the book of Joel Chapter 2: verses 25-26: 25. And I will restore to you the years that the locust hath eaten, the cankerworm, and the caterpillar, and the palmerworm, my great army which I sent among you. 26. And ye shall eat in plenty, and be satisfied, and praise the name of the Lord your God, that hath dealt wondrously with you: and my people shall never be ashamed. Now we see conclusively why the devil doesn't want prophets in the churches, nor to know the type of anointing that they operate under. Prophets operate under a creative- anointing. They have the ability to cancel the plans of the devil. The cankerworm, caterpillar, and the palmerworm are typologies of demons. In the book of Micah Chapter 7: verse 15-17: 15. According to the days of thy coming out of the land of Egypt will I show unto him marvelous things. 16. The nations shall see and be confounded at all their might: they shall lay their hand upon their mouth, their ears shall be deaf. 17. They shall lick the dust like a serpent, they shall move out of their holes like worms of the earth: they shall be afraid of the Lord our God, and shall fear because of thee. Prophets come to confound you to believe and to trust in God. Their words shall cancel the plans of the devil over your life. Once the prophetic word is spoken by the mouth of the prophet, then the word of the Lord can cancel your past, and create life in the now for your future. The scripture says that the nations shall lay their hand upon their mouth. They shall be astonied and amazed at the accuracy of the word of the Lord. Their ears shall be deaf which means they really can't believe the confirmation of the word of the Lord. The prophets will leave no stone unturned. They nations shall lick the dust like a serpent. Once the word of the Lord is spoken by the mouth of the prophet they will want to bless the prophet. To lick the dust like a serpent means servants hood. They shall want to bless the prophet. You have those who are prophet-teachers. They are prophets but their main area in which they flow in is in teaching. You have those who are not prophets, but they are teachers. These teachers are theologians in which God has given them the grace to flow heavily into the word of God. Evangelist usually flows in the prophetic. That does not mean they are prophets. They could be a prophet, but just choose to use the title evangelist. They know that they are witnesses of the Lord Jesus Christ, as we all are, and should be witnesses for Christ. Dreams and visions can come from the soul, the demonic, or the Holy Spirit. We must be able to discern where the dream or visions came from. In mastery we begin to put away childish things and walk into maturity, to discern good from evil. Remember everything that looks and sound good does not means it is good. The devil knows how to imitate God and the things of God. Remember the jezebel spirit comes with all power, signs, and lying wonders. Do you see how deceptive this spirit can be. Not only does this spirit come in power-authority, and signs-of God, but this spirits deception is lying wonders and imitations. It's main purpose is to get you to turn from God to fall for the bait of satan, and the consequences for allowing this spirit to operate is that God will cause great destruction. God will place you in a bed, and those that commit adultery with you into great tribulation, and also God will kill your children with death. Meaning actual death and your children; meaning not only your birth children, but those that you care about. There is so much more in dealing with the prophets. Dreams and visions volume 2: will go more into detail. The group that I have called Battle Ax Watchman at the Gates: is a group primarily dealing with the prophets. I have a group called Skies Da limit Seers, Seerology, Realm of the Seer, and these groups deal with the seers. I have Prophetic Detectives, Prophetic Inner Circle, The Martyr of the Prophets and much more online that deals with the prophetic. Let us examine the book of Ezekiel Chapter 1: verse 1:Now it came to pass in the thirtieth year, in the fourth month, in the fifth day of the month, as I was among the captives by the river of Chebar, that the heavens were opened, and I saw visions of God. As I begin to examine this literature in verse 1: I heard the Lord speak to me today: 4.8.2013: Monday: that prophets have the uncanny ability to cause the heavens to open up in the midst of scarcity. They have the ability to change economic crisis. Ezekiel Chapter 1: verse 3: The word of the Lord came expressly unto Ezekiel the priest, the son of Buzi, in the land of the Chaldeans by the river Chebar; and the hand of the Lord was there upon him. not only was Ezekiel a priest but Ezekiel was a seer, even though he was a prophet. What makes him different from your ordinary prophet is that he carried a heavier grace, known as, sanctification. The sanctification was the priesthood anointing. Your prophets will have open heavens, as well as your seers. Prophets go into the inner court while your seers go behind the veil. The priesthood anointing is a greater death-walk that a seer has to go into more than the prophet. In the book of numbers Chapter 12: verse 6: And he said, Hear now my words: If there be a prophet among you, I the Lord will make myself known unto him in a vision, and will speak unto him in a dream. Seers operate in a greater stream of the prophetic impartation. They are more pictorial than the prophet. God makes himself known unto the seers, which is a prophet in a vision, which means in many manifestations of the Spirit. While the prophet operates more in dreams, which is the similitude of the Lord; (dark speeches). Prophets operate by using parables, riddles, mysteries, and proverbs. These are dreams that God use to speak to the prophet in the prophetic flow of dreams. When the seer and the prophet work together, as they are led by the Lord to do so the miraculous will begin to happen suddenly. Seers can be apostles, prophets, evangelists, teachers, pastors, or elders. Although they may not use the name seer does not mean that they are not seers. A lot of them choose not to use the name seer, like some choose not to use the name elder, or apostle. Even though they may be elders, or apostles. This is why we must be very careful who we entertain because some are actually angels in disguise. Remember that clergy names do not mean anything. Even though I am an Apostle I am a servant of the Lord all the days of my life. Titles mean nothing to me. Yes we must respect titles, and clergy names, but we must be careful, and try the spirit by the spirit of God within us. Now the seer anointing can come upon a prophet, even though God has not called all prophets to be seers. If a person desires to be a seer God will give them the grace to walk into that office. I'm here to tell you that there is a price to pay. Everyone wants something from God for free, but no one wants to pay the price. You have to go through something in order to receive anything from the Lord.

Chapter 10

Spiritual-Warfare

There is a force working behind the scenes called spiritual-wickedness working in the churches releasing witchcraft in the churches. Those who are in spiritual-witchcraft are double-minded and very unstable. Their mission is to build their kingdom and to control someone else. Their mission is to manipulate others into doing their bidding. They are devils trying to control and manipulate people to do their will. These spirits bring chaos and turmoil wherever they go. When people don't know if they are coming or going, know that it's a form of witchcraft, because they are unstable. A sign that someone is under the influence of witchcraft is that if you're talking to them and they start doing other things. When they walk away this is a sign of witchcraft. A spirit of witchcraft will do everything necessary to get unto you. There is a spiritual-wickedness in the earth that is very religious, and this spirit is mainly in the church and wants to release witch-craft in the church. Bishop George Bloomer wrote a book called witch-craft in the pews. There is witch-craft in the pews all over the globe. There was a movie that I saw called the possession in which this man bought his daughter a big box, but he did not know that a demon was in the box. So his daughter ends up opening up the box, and she became possessed by the demonic spirit. We must be very careful about our environments. We must watch and examine everything very carefully so that we don't entertain the demonic, such as things dealing with the occult, and soul-ties. Warning against soul-ties. The bible says in the book of Deuteronomy Chapter 7: verses 1-5: 1. When the Lord thy God shall bring thee into the land whither thou goest to possess it, and hath cast out many nations before thee, the Hittites, and the Girgashites, and the Amorites, and the Canaanites, and the Perizzites, and the Hivites, and the Jebusites, seven nations greater and mightier than thou; 2. And when the Lord thy God shall deliver them before thee; thou shalt smite them, and utterly destroy them; thou shalt make no covenant with them, nor shew mercy unto them: 3. Neither shalt thou make marriages with them; thy daughter thou shalt not give unto his son, nor his daughter shalt thou take unto thy son. 4. For they will turn away thy son from following me that they may serve other Gods: so will the anger of the Lord be kindled against you, and destroy thee suddenly. 5. But thus shall ye deal with them; ye shall destroy their altars, and break down their images, and cut down their groves, and burn their graven images with fire. Beloved it takes the power of prayer to overthrow the works of the devil. The seven nations are a typology of the demonic. They are people that are possessed with demonic-spirits. One of the warnings that the Lord give us is not to make covenant (friendships) with people outside of Christianity. One of the demonic- setups in the body of Christ is that if a man, or a woman of God marries outside of their Christian-religion there will be chaos. When the woman has children even though you are a Christian your spouse shall teach the children opposite of the word of God. They shall contaminate them by leaving them confused with teaching of false religions. God tells us not to make marriages with those outside of the Christian-religion because they will turn thy children from the Lord. Why does the scripture say in verse 4: for they will turn away thy son from following me? The answer is the reason why God says so because God created man. The woman was made for the man. No I'm not saying that males are better than women no not all. There is an order just like there is a prophetic-order. The males are suppose to be the leaders in their families as they should be the leaders in their marriage. The purpose of having children is to train and raise them to serve God. There are many women of God who are married unto a men who are not a Christian. We have so many men of God who are married unto a women who are not Christian. I'm here to tell you that you will have hell on your hands if you marry outside of yours, but God does not approve same sex marriage. You can marry a nationality that is different from yours. When you marry outside of your religion you bring destruction upon yourself.

This is an avenue how demons can come into your life by the influence of soul-ties. A primary example of how the demonic can come into your life is found in the book of 1st Kings Chapter 11: verses 1-6: 1.but king Solomon loved many strange women, together with the daughter of pharaoh, women of the Moabites, ammonites, Edomites, Zidonians, and Hittites; 2. Of the nations concerning which the Lord said unto the children of Israel, ye shall not go in to them, neither shall they come in unto you: for surely they will turn away your heart after their Gods: Solomon clave unto these in love. 3. And he had seven hundred wives, princesses, and three hundred concubines: and his wives turned away his heart. 4. For it came to pass, when Solomon was old, that his wives turned away his heart after other Gods: and his heart was not perfect with the Lord his God, as was the heart of David his father. 5. For Solomon went after Ashtoreth the Goddess of the Zidonians, and after Milcom the abomination of the ammonites. 6. And Solomon did evil in the sight of the Lord, and went not fully after the Lord, as did David his father. King Solomon loved many strange women, but the strange women were not holy women of God because they were unusual, nothing that Solomon was accustomed too. They served others Gods. These Gods were demons in disguise. The significance of the other Gods was that the demonic was tied unto these Gods. Even today the demonic operates the same way. The purpose of these other Gods is to turn the people of God from the Lord. The devil knows that he can't stop you so he and his army set-up traps to destroy you. You have to realize that the devil and the realm of the demoniac have been here since the beginning. They have been watching and observing the human race from the beginning. The reason why Jesus says that the devil has been a murderer from the beginning is, because of the war in heaven. Satans' job is to steal, kill, and to destroy. So Satan tricked eve into convincing Adam to eat the forbidden fruit. Satan is a murderer because the same thing that caused him to fall he convinced man that they were not Gods. There were other people here in the earth before God created Adam and Eve. These people were not like Adam and Eve. They were created in God's image, but not in his likeness. Satan was to teach the angels and the other type of man to obey God to praise and worship God. His job was to take the praise and the worship unto God but something happened unto Satan. He was so fascinated with God and his glory that he deceived his own self. This can be found in the book of Ezekiel Chapter 28: verses 12-19: Witchcraft-is manipulation; to gain control over another by any means necessary. Using the word of God for selfish gain. Pharmaceuticals are witchcraft also. If its use to control your mind other than the spirit of God its witchcraft. Rebellion, and sorcery is witchcraft. The word Wicca is the chanting, using object to summons, to seek power other than God by summoning the demonic realm. Galatians Chapter 5: verses 19-21: 19. Now the works of the flesh are manifest, which are these; adultery, fornication, uncleanness, lasciviousness,

20. Idolatry, witchcraft, hatred, variance, emulations, wrath, strife, seditions, heresies, 21. Envying, murders, drunkenness, retellings, and such like: of the which I tell you before, as I have also told you in time past, that they which do such things shall not inherit the kingdom of God. All these are forms of witchcraft. These forms of witchcraft are signs that people are under the influence of the demonic.

The Armor of God:

The scripture says in the book of Ephesians Chapter 6: verses 10-18: 10.Finally, my brethren, be strong in the Lord, and in the power of his might. 11. Put on the whole armour of God, that ye may be able to stand against the wiles of the devil. 12. For we wrestle not against flesh and blood, but against principalities, against powers, against the rulers of the darkness of this world, against spiritual wickedness in high places. 13. Wherefore take unto you the whole armour of God, that ye may be able to withstand in the evil day, and having done all, to stand. 14. Stand therefore, having your loins girt about with truth, and having on the breastplate of righteousness; 15. And your feet shod with the preparation of the gospel of peace; 16. Above all, taking the shield of faith, wherewith ye shall be able to quench all the fiery darts of the wicked. 17. And take the helmet of salvation, and the sword of the spirit, which is the word of God: 18. Praying always with all prayer and supplication in the spirit, and watching thereunto with all perseverance and supplication for all saints; To be strong in the Lord is not enough. We must also walk in the power of Gods might. The power of Gods might is trusting God even when you don't understand. We understand that faith comes by hearing and hearing by the word of God. Romans 10:17: We as born again believers must trust in the power of his might that if God said it, then we must rest assure that God is going to perform everything that he said in his word. God will perform everything that he has promised you. Even when we get weary God will give us more strength to stand and move forward. Isaiah 40: 28-31: the power of his might is the manifestation of the spirit. Mark 16: 15-18; Mt 28: 18-20; Joshua 1:5. There are many other scriptures that we can use as a reference but these are to name a few. The purpose of the armor: of God is to stand against the whiles, schemes, tactics, devices, traps, onslaughts, and weapons of the devil. 2nd Corinthians 2:11. The devil and his army will come at you with all of their arsenal to try and stop you, block you, hinder you, derail you, detour you. The whole purpose of these attacks is to try and make you quit serving God. Territorial Devils. Daniel 10: 11-13. We do not fight against people but we fight against despotisms, against the powers, against the master-spirits who are the world rulers of this present darkness. against spiritual-forces of wickedness in heavenly places. There are spirits like in the book of Daniel Chapter 10: 11-13 that do not like you. They do not want the word of God to go forth into that nation.

Whenever you go into a nation you will fight against principalities. We are wrestling with powers behind the scene. We can't see them with our natural eyes. You have to see them in the spirit known, as the realm of the spirit. That's why you have to be careful who you have with you in your inner-circle because many of your friends may not be equipped to handle what you are about to go up against. If you recall the video on YouTube.com Bishop Eddie L. Long did a sermon called Leading While Bleeding. When you get time check it out if you haven't watched it. If you do not have people who are close to you who do not watch in the spirit to cover and, to pray for you, and to watch your back then these people can be tools of the devil to work against you. Even if they are good people they can still be used by the devil to attack you. I have experienced this before many times. People will be attracted to your anointing and they will care less about you. These are mockers, scorners going after their ungodly lust. There are many in the churches of God who are not saved, and you have those who are saved but are not filled with the Holy Ghost. Meaning that they were once filled with the spirit of God but were turned over unto a reprobate mind back over unto the devil. They have vexed and have grieved the spirit of God. The bible talks about how the wicked one satan comes to steal the word of God out of our hearts. Matthew Chapter 13: verses 18-19: 18. Hear ye therefore the parable of the sower. 19. When any one heareth the word of the kingdom, and understandeth it not, then cometh the wicked one, and catcheth away that which was sown in his heart. This is he which received seed by the way side. When we are in warfare we must be careful about Gods word that is in our hearts. The devil and his army want to steal the word of God out of our hearts by fear. Fear is having faith in death, and faith is taking God at his word. That if God said it that he will do it. Satans trap is to get you to believe a lie, rather the then word of God. There are territorial spirits; princes ruling over lands. They are like birds on a power line that when you come into their territorial-spirits they are coming after you to try and stop you from doing the work of God. They are all over the world. They strongly work over governments. The strategy of the devil is to take out everyone from receiving Jesus Christ from hearing the good news which is the word of God. So the devil is very strategic and influences leaders to turn from God. This is the devils-tactics which is jezebel. To possess and oppress leadership in order to control the masses under the leader. And just like God chooses and uses leaders to govern the people. The devil does the same thing, but for corruption to destroy nations. So many people are praying for Gods-will to manifest here in the earth-realm, but we need to get to the root of the problem. The root of the problem is to seek the Lord in prayer to find out who do the devil mainly use as his p.i.m.p.s. to dominate and to control to control nations. The answer is governments. God has raised up an army of vigilant-soldiers apostles to pull down the princes that are over territories. The prophets will battle and warfare against demons, but your apostle will battle against fallen-angels; which are princes that rules and govern over territories. People are just praying for change and for things they desire, but we must pray that Gods-will manifest unto us We are to seek the Lord in prayer and God will download unto us the wisdom, knowledge, and understanding that we need to walk in our dominion ship. Ephesians Chapter 6: verse 10: finally, my brethren, be strong in the Lord, and in the power of his might to be strong in the Lord is having faith in God despite how things look, sound, and feel that is contrary of Gods' word. the power of his might is talking about the apostolic and the prophetic. the scripture says that in the book of Ephesians Chapter 2: verses 20-22: 20. And are built upon the foundation of the apostles and prophets, Jesus Christ himself being the chief corner stone; 21. In whom all the building fitly framed together groweth unto a holy temple in the Lord: 22. In whom ye also are built together for a habitation of God through the spirit. the church is built upon the apostolic and the prophetic. Jesus Christ is the chief cornerstone which means that he has placed the apostolic and the prophetic, as the head to establish government order for his body. The apostle will operate in all the gift of the Spirit. The apostles operate in miracles. The prophets operate in a creative-anointing. The miracles are found in the book of Luke Chapter 4: verse 18-19: 18. The spirit of the Lord is upon me, because he hath anointed me to preach the gospel to the poor; he hath sent me to heal the brokenhearted, to preach deliverance to the captives, and recovering of sight to the blind, to set at liberty them that are bruised, 19. To preach the acceptable year of the Lord. All saint(Christians) can operate in deliverance and healing, as it has been commissioned in the book of Mark Chapter 16: but the apostle has and operate in a master-anointing. Their assignment is not for the weak in heart. The apostle is going to carry more weight than the prophet, pastor, teacher, and evangelist. The apostle is the battle-ax: the covering and protection of Gods-sheep. The apostle is the c.e.o. owner of a business, or businesses. The apostle can operate in all the gifts of the spirit. The apostle can operate as the apostle, prophet, pastor, teacher, and the evangelist. The problem with the body of Christ is the church, even though the church is like the body of Christ and yet is different. The apostle holds the body together rule ring over the churches that God has given the apostle to govern. The apostle mentors, trains, develops, nurture, instruct, discipline, and teaches their pastors that are over churches to feed the sheep with knowledge and understanding. Although some of the pastors that are over a church who is under the master-teacher which is the apostle may in fact be an apostle in the making. The power of Gods-might is believing and trusting God no matter what. This is one on one with you and God. the 2nd phase of the power of Gods might it the installment: of the apostle. because even though you have the pastor, teacher, prophet, and the evangelist without the apostle you will be ensnared, deceived, and caught in satans-deceptions which is jezebel. That's why satan hates the prophetic-ministry and the apostolic-ministry more than she hates the other three. because Ephesians Chapter 2: verse 20: let us know that the body is built upon the ministry of the apostolic and the prophetic. the prophets and the apostles could never get alone because it was not time decades ago. the pastors, teachers which are theologians, and the evangelist which are the soul-winners shall mightily increase and accomplish much because of the ministry of the apostles and the prophets. anyone who does not lead someone unto the Lord Jesus Christ to receive salvation is a false-prophet. and the apostolic-ministry: is to confront the false-prophets. false-prophets: are only after fitly-lucre. they do not care for Gods sheep as stated in the book of John Chapter 10: verse 12: but he that is an hireling, and not the shepherd, whose own the sheep are not, seeth the wolf coming, and leaveth the sheep, and fleeth: and the wolf catcheth them, and scattereth the sheep. there are many hirelings in the churches all over the world. and they have come in disguise smiling, quoting scriptures, pretending to be nice. pretending to love Gods people. these boast and brag about themselves and the works that they have done. but God allow these wolves to come into the body for the elect to know they systems and strategy of the devil which is jezebel. to turn a person away from God unto lie. which is the word delusion. but these false-prophets: wolves: have and shall fall into Gods net. which when the word of God is spoken by these false prophets at that time when they speak Gods word they are judged by God. these are filthy-dreamers; deceivers having a form of Godliness, but denying the power of God. That is why when you know someone is false pretending to be a Christian; pretending to be a preacher of Christ you judge them by discernment. They are in danger of judgment, because when they minister the word of God with wrong -intention; with wrong-motives they are at that time judged for the blasphemy against the Holy-Ghost. God will give them space to repent of their deeds, but after a time he will place these liars, false-prophets upon a greet bed of affliction and will kill them and their love ones with death until they repent. Christ said that all churches shall know that it is he which searcheth the reins and hearts: and he will give unto every one of you according to your works. Jesus Christ being the chief cornerstone: chief architect meaning that it is established that he has placed the apostles and the prophets to build and to establish the church within his body. This does not mean that the pastors, teachers, and the ministry of the evangelist is excluded. We are all one body and we need each other. In these last days the ministry of the apostolic and the ministry of the prophetic will be the fortress, and tower to protect the pastors, teachers, and the ministry of the evangelist. while they pastors, teachers, and the evangelist protect Gods sheep. Jeremiah Chapter 6: verse 27: I have set thee for a tower and a fortress among my people, that thou mayest know and try their way. Each preacher is a fortress, and a tower, which means that he should have given you a word from the bible that established who you are and your ministry. **God** has given you, as a fortress of protection against the demoniacs and against all weapons. God has all of those angels that he have with you, and around you to watch, guard, and to protect you at all times. He has made you a tower by setting you high above all the nations of the world, which means the spirit of discernment to operate not just in knowledge, but in wisdom and understanding. That we should not live, nor think like the world, but we are here to save generations from destroying themselves. 1st Corinthians Chapter 1: verse 21: For after that in the wisdom of God the world by wisdom knew not God, it pleased God by the foolishness of preaching to save them that believe. The armor of God is, also the 5 fold ministry that God has inducted, and instituted in the churches to disciple, teach, train, nurture, instruct, and to develop the saint of God. The perfection which is the development and perfection, and maturity of the saint of God.

Key point # 42:
I hear the word of the Lord saying that I am altering, shifting, and changing the divine-order of the apostles and the prophets. I am causing my servants to come together in the last-days to do mightily works in my kingdom. For I am causing a union of fellowship to be birthed amongst warrior-spirits to battle-ax, tear-down, up-root, pull-down, and to destroy the works of the devil. For I am exposing witches, and warlocks

in these last days who are prophetic-witches in disguise. For yea, saith the Lord for these witches shall get sick and shall die. For they deceive my people into believing lies and fables and have turned them away from the truth, as in the days of old, even now, I am raising up an army of the apostles and prophets to join to confront demonic-opposition in the churches. For I am about to expose these magicians, wizards, clairvoyant are workers of iniquity who are false prophets; wolves in sheep-clothing. Many shall instantly die and give up the ghost for the blasphemy against the Holy-Ghost. I am purging my house saith the Lord. For those who do not lead the nations unto me this is a sign that they are false. Ezekiel 34:2: Son of man, prophesy against the shepherds of Israel, prophesy, and say unto them, thus saith the Lord God unto the shepherds; woe be to the shepherds of Israel that do feed themselves! should not the shepherds feed the flocks?

Spiritual-Warfare: is you engaging in battle against the powers that will try and block, stop, and hinder the kingdom of God from manifesting in the earth-realm. It's you the believer taking the kingdom by force. The Kingdom cannot be taken by the Kingdom of heaven. The Kingdom can only be taken by the Kingdom of God; which is the power. The Kingdom of heaven is a place, as in reference to the mind: (consciousness). The Kingdom of heaven refers to the spirit. As God reveals and down- loads unto us wisdom, knowledge, and understanding we therefore seek him in prayer on what to do, and how to do it. We do not fight, not battle against people, but against the powers; which is the authority that princes: (fallen-angels); (demons); and (unclean-spirits): have.

We are to battle against the influence that they have on mankind. All the devil can do it to try and influence your mind. The devil doesn't know any more than what you tell him.

Witchcraft-Probing:

When people are under demonic influence they will try and ask your questions, trying to probe questions out of your soul in order to find out your vulnerability. They want to know your weakness in order to make you a slave of them; therefore when they make you their slave you have become at that time jezebels-eunuch. The devil knows that whosoever you sit under you will become just like them. So when we look at the high places we understand that its talking about the mind, but the high places also are in reference unto people in authority. The 2nd phase of high places in people is known, as authority. Princes which are fallen-angels using demons(nephalim): to possess, or oppress someone in a great position. As an apostle of the Lord Jesus Christ I seek the Lord in prayer and fasting so that I may know the spirit and who the spirit in operating in. So that I may come against these territorial spirits in the name of Jesus. Witch-craft is manipulation, sorcery to try and probe into someone's life. This is divination which is the foresight to see into the without the spirit of God. The churches are infested with witch-craft; witches who are in prophetic-disguise. Jesus said that in the book of John Chapter 16: verse 13: Howbeit when he, the spirit of truth, is come, he will guide you into all truth: for he shall not speak of himself; but whatsoever he shall hear, that shall he speak: and he will shew you things to come. So the spirit of God comes to guide us into all truth. We must be able to see through the lies and deception of the devil by Gods spirit. We are to at all times walk into the truth of Gods word. Ephesians 4:14: That we henceforth be no more children, tossed to and fro, and carried about with every wind of doctrine, by the sleight of men, and cunning craftiness, whereby they lie in wait to deceive; We see witch- craft can be in the form of seduction, which is the word cunning. It's like the word con man, or con artist. That witch-craft probing is an art of deception, art of seduction, to bait its victim to make them a eunuch. What is the old saying that people use to say back in the day? That birds of a feather flock together. I use as my motto that for wheresoever you're going that's who you're connected too. And whosoever you're connected too that where you're going. You will become just like your master or mentor. You are what you eat. We must be very careful who we allow to be over us. We must not jump from church to church just because we see someone that we like. We must at all times be led by the spirit of God, because many do not discern the body of the Lord they become sick. We are to discern the body of the Lord by obeying Gods voice. Many are walking in deception and do not know it. Jezebels main purpose is to steal, kill, and to destroy; to try and block, stop, and hinder the move of God in the lives of people. That's why we see so many dry churches where the Lord is not there. Matthew Chapter 24: verses 23-28: 23. Then if any man shall say unto you, lo, here is Christ, or there; believe it not. 24. For there shall arise false Christ's, and false prophets, and shall shew great signs and wonders; insomuch that, if it were possible, they shall deceive the very elect. 25. Behold, I have told you before. 26. Wherefore if they shall say unto you, behold, he is in the desert; go not forth: behold, he is in the secret chambers; believe it not. 27. For as the lightning cometh out of the east, and shineth even unto the west; so shall also the coming of the son of man be. 28. For wheresoever the carcass is, there will the eagles be gathered together. There shall arise false Christ's which are jezebels eunuchs slaves under demonic influence. False prophets are not just people who say that they are preachers, but they will be in literally every profession trying to deceive even the very elect of God. Remember as the scripture saith in the book of 2nd Thessalonians Chapter 2: verse 9-11: 9.Even him, whose coming is after the working of satan with all power and signs and lying wonders, 10. And with all deceivableness of unrighteousness in them that perish; because they received not the love of the truth, that they might be saved. 11. And for this cause God shall send them strong delusion, that they should believe a lie: The working of satan is with all power, signs of God, and lying wonders. Just because people say that they are of God does not mean that they are from God, because jezebel which is the arsenal weaponry of the devil can operate in all power of God, and signs of God. This spirit is deceptive and operates in lying wonders. This is a deception of the devil to turn people away from God to serve other Gods. It's not the power of God that is deceiving people. It's the signs. If the signs that a person performs does not draw and lead a person unto Jesus Christ, then they are false. To make sure of who are, and what spirit they are operating under ask the Holy Spirit within you who shall guide you into all truth. The scripture says that this spirit comes with all power and signs. The signs are the power, and the power is the signs. What makes the power false, or a lying wonder? The jezebel spirit will not lead you, or someone to Christ. This lying prophetic spirit will lead you unto themselves in order to get you to serve another god, and to not serve God the father. The devil know the word of God, and that Gods word will not come back void. So satan uses the word of God for his advantage. let's look at the book of Isaiah Chapter 55: verse 11: So shall my word be that goeth forth out of my mouth: it shall not return unto me void, but it shall accomplish that which I please, and it shall prosper in the thing whereto I sent it. We see that satan is not ignorant of the word of God. satan knows that Gods word will not come back void. We have a lot of false Christ's and false prophets who are using Gods word for the wrong purpose. They are only after filthy lucre. They do not care about you. They only care about themselves. These are hirelings. These are jezebels eunuchs. 1st timothy Chapter 3: verse 3:Not given to wine, no striker, not greedy of filthy lucre; but patient, not a brawler, not covetous; This spirit is very greedy for worldly gain, and is very covetous. This spirit is very crafty and can camouflage. This spirit disguises itself to make you think it's of God, but God will reveal and show you the true motive of the person who is operating in jezebel. What is jezebel? Jezebel is a spirit of rebellion, defiance against God. A disobedient spirit. this spirit will not submit unto authority, but will rebel who it gets its way. this spirit targets and tries to hijack the prophetic-ministry of the true prophets of God. jezebel assignment is the church is to seduce and to deceive the apostle in the church. Now let me tell you that if the leader in the church is not an apostle it does not mean that they are not the leader in the church overseeing the flock of God. Some actually go by the name elder Bishop, or Pastor. I mentioned apostle because jezebels assignment is to kill the leaders in the church so that the people will be scattered. I have seen this spirit in operation many times. I have seen women of God constantly try and to seduce the male leadership in the churches on many occasions. I remember in the year 2003 that when I was a deacon that a woman tried to come to the pulpit to try and talk to the pastor. the Lord opened up my eyes and I saw the spirit that she was operating under and she tried her best to get the pastors attention and I stopped her from walking on the pulpit. I escorted her out of the church. because what she was doing was out of order; the spirit was totally out of control. and as the bishop was preaching she just kept screaming and trying to ask the bishop something. the word of God tells us that in the book of 1st Corinthians Chapter 14: verse 40: let all things be done decently and in order. If things are not done in decency, and in order as proper protocol by your leader in the church, then you are out of order. You are operating in a spirit of disobedience if you go against your leadership. Jesus said and you shall know them by their fruits. Our job as children of God is to pray for them that they change from their evil ways. Remember that's not them that's a spirit that has them under the influence to be disobedient. We love the hell out of them, until the hell leaves and flees from them. 1st Corinthians Chapter 14: verses 32-33: 32. And the spirits of the prophets are subject to the prophets. 33. For God is not the author of confusion, but of peace, as in all churches of the saints. We can prophesy and reveal mysteries all the time, but if someone is constantly giving a word of the Lord, then they are not from God. If someone tells you to give them money for a word of the Lord they are not of God. So many people are falling for this deception of satan. The spirit of the prophets are subject to the prophets; which means that the spirit upon you; whether you be an apostle, prophet, pastor, teacher, or an evangelist is subject unto you. Many operate in divination, and do not know that are operating in the demonic. This is a sign and a warning that many are operating in jezebel. Just because someone gives you a word does not mean that they are from God. The devil and his demons know the word of God also, as a matter of fact the devil knows the word of God better than any of us. I have seen true prophets of God become ensnared in the deception of jezebel. Their prophetic ministry becomes hijacked without them knowing, and the spirit of jezebel releases a spirit of confusion upon its victim.

Witch-craft confusion: The spirit of jezebel will release a spirit of confusion upon its victim.

1. These are the signs: of witch-craft confusion: these people will forget who they are.
2. They will always be lost and confused.
3. They will always try and start something and never completing what they are doing.
4. If you ask them a question a lot of times they will immediately try and change the question, or they will immediately walk away.
5. They will be serving other Gods. They will not glorify God, which means that they are always sad, depressed, walking in the spirit of fear, they are constantly tormented, and they are always blaming people for what happened to them. They do not walk in the fruit of the Spirit.
6. They are vain in their imaginations These are gossipers, idolaters, their hearts are foolish and darkened.

These are the main signs of Witch-craft Confusion that is released against the mind of its victim. This is the venom of jezebel.

How does jezebel lure you into her trap?

Jezebel which is a warfare, or strategy of the devil is to find you when you are most vulnerable. She lures you into her trap by witch-craft probing you. She does it by asking you numerous question to try, and to find out your weaknesses. She loves to find out a person vulnerability so that she may bait in her victim. I have a group online called Mark: of the Beast: Warlock: in which this is a pharaoh-spirit that is known, as the spirit of Ahab. This person could have started out good, but was ensnared into jezebels deception; thus making this male prophet, or male child of God a eunuch which is a slave. So the anointing that is on that person's life cannot be contaminated, but their soul(mind, will, and emotions): can be altered, changed and corrupt. This person becomes a slave(eunuch): of jezebel and they will think that they are hearing directly from God. They will think that they are seeing dreams and visions from the Lord. Also you can tell that this person is a slave(eunuch): of jezebel is that they are constantly prophesying all the time. They shall always have a word for you, but they themselves are in a ditch. Revelation Chapter 3: verse 17: Because thou sayest, I am rich, and increased with goods, and have need of nothing; and knowest not that thou art wretched, and miserable, and poor, and blind, and naked: the spirit: of jezebel: blinds its victim from the truth.

1. Witch-craft Probing. jezebel probes by searching out your weaknesses(vulnerability): so that she may ensnare and trap you to make you her(eunuch): slave.

2. Jezebel seeks to find those who have been (hurt, wounded, scarred, betrayed, and rejected): the main ones who have been rejected are the ones jezebel is mainly coming after to lure them into her trap.

3. Jezebel seeks those who are in isolation who are away from their leadership in the church, so that she may make them her slave(eunuchs); to gain control as their new leader. Prophets are mainly jezebels-target, because jezebel knows that the prophets are the (gate-keepers): of the (sheep- flock: of God): Therefore if she can lure away, and remove the (prophet): from their post, then she has a greater change of destroying them. At the same time since the prophet is removed from their (post): she will send her false-prophets(eunuch): in to (deceive, wound, scare, hurt, and to scatter the sheep):

4. Jezebel seeks those who are impatient. You see satan knows the word of God, and that with the word of God comes tribulation and patience. Jezebel sends her (false-prophets): (wolves: in sheeps-clothing): coming with all

(power, signs, and lying-wonders): to (lure, ensnare, seduce, manipulate, and to trap): her victim. Luke Chapter 8: verse 15: But that on the good ground are they, which in an honest and good heart, having heard the word, keep it, and bring forth fruit with patience. Luke Chapter 21: verse 19: In your patience possess ye your souls. why patience? Because in patience God is talking to you, and revealing unto you his divine-will. Bishop Young use to tell me, Bishop A, Joann Branch, Pastor Christine to always be patient. Patience also causes your enemy to throw in the towel. Patience is where you will see the (arsenal, weaponry, devices, onslaught, traps, schemes, and whiles: of the devil): Patience will cause you to (seer): in the (spirit of discernment): Patience will strengthen you when you are weak, as you seek God in prayer.

5. Jezebel can form (soul-ties): with you by (witch-craft probing); that when she finds your weaknesses and plays on your (emotions): Like she really cares, then she has you. She forms (soul-ties): with you without you even knowing, and she does this through (witch-craft probing); searching your (soul: mind, will, and emotions): to attach her spirit under yours by (releasing): a (spirit of witch-craft): upon you; therefore creating a (soul-tie): a (bond): with you.

Who does jezebel uses to ensnare and trap you?

Isaiah Chapter 54: verse 17: Behold, they shall surely gather together, but not by me: whosoever shall gather together against thee shall fall for thy sake.

1. When jezebel senses fear, or that she's being infiltrated she will send in her servants (slaves: eunuch): to try and (infiltrate): you by (camouflage): by having her (eunuchs): pretend to be nice. They will pretend to befriend you, by pretending to have your best interest in mind.

2. Jezebel uses your past against you to try and make you afraid. She does this to get you to be fearful so that she may (probe): you to know your (vulnerabilities): so that she may release (witch- craft confusion): upon you to cause a (soul-tie): (bond): with you.

3. Jezebel will use your (family, friends, associates, people from your past): in order to (tear): you down so that she may come when you're most (vulnerable): to (probe): you in order to make a (soul-tie): with you; to (control): you.

4. Jezebel will use the word of God to (deceive): you into thinking that she is from God. She will try and make you believe that she is the (Christ): in order to (bait): you in by you letting down your (guards). Just because someone claims to know the word of God does not mean that they are from God. The devil knows the word of

God better than any of us. The scripture tells us to try the spirit by the spirit. 1st John Chapter 4: verse 1: Beloved, believe not every spirit, but try the spirits whether they are of God: because many false prophets are gone out into the world. we try the spirit people are operating in by the (spirit: of discernment):

5. Jezebel will try and lure you into her trap by playing on your emotions. She will pretend to cry and actually have false-tears, pretending to be sad, pretending to be depressed, pretending to be lonely in order to draw you unto her, so that you may have compassion for her. Then when she sees that you have compassion for her she will, then use your emotions to connect with your soul to (manipulate): you to be her (slave):

6. If jezebel is operating in a woman then she will try and lure you into having sex with her to form a (soul-tie), because once the physical-intimacy happens their spirits will become one. This can come through A. pornography on TV, or online. B. by pornography magazines, pornography books. C. sex toys. Deity can come through the eye-gate, ear-gate, and by physical contact by someone physically seducing you by touching, feeling, and rubbing on you. Jezebel will even be bold enough to come at a married man having no conscience of what she wants to do, is about to do, and does not care about

destroying the married man's life. e. Jezebel will also try and seduce a woman, even though a woman may be operating in jezebel. She can seduce even females into being (lesbians; gay): She's play on a woman's emotions who have been cheated on, hurt, betrayed, lied too, and used by a man. Jezebel will play on a woman's emotions to bait her in. f. If the jezebel-spirit is operating in a male, then this is not just a witch but a (warlock): commonly operating in the churches all over the world. This (warlock-spirit): is known, as the (pharaoh-spirit, or the Ahab-spirit): the names just changed over time. It's all the same. This (warlock-spirit): can only operate in a man and is more powerful, and stronger than a female witch. The female jezebel does not work alone, but is under the (command): of her (master): which is (pharaoh: warlock, or known as, Ahab): The female jezebel gets her (orders, and instructions): from her (master): which is (Ahab): to get, trap, and ensnare more people into becoming the warlocks (slaves: eunuch): The bible says that in the book: of Deuteronomy Chapter 7: verses 1-6: 1. When the Lord thy God shall bring thee into the land whither thou goest to possess it, and hath cast out many nations before thee, the Hittites, and the Girgashites, and the Amorites, and the Canaanites, and the Perizzites, and the Hivites, and the Jebusites, seven nations greater and mightier than thou; 2. And when the Lord thy God shall deliver them before thee; thou shalt smite them, and utterly destroy them; thou shalt make no covenant with them, nor shew mercy unto them: 3. Neither shalt thou make marriages with them; thy daughter thou shalt not give unto his son, nor his daughter shalt thou take unto thy son. 4. For they will turn away thy son from following me, that they may serve other Gods: so will the anger of the Lord be kindled against you, and destroy thee suddenly. 5. But thus shall ye deal with them; ye shall destroy their altars, and break down their images, and cut down their groves, and burn their graven images with fire. 6. For thou art an holy people unto the Lord thy God: the Lord thy God hath chosen thee to be a special people unto himself, above all people that are upon the face of the earth.

7. Jezebel will use someone in the church to touch you while you are in the spirit; whether you are sitting down, standing up, or slain in the spirit. We must be very careful who we allow to pray for us, and to pray over us. You must be very careful who you allow to be in your inner-circle, because everyone who say that they are for you are not for you. I have seen many times someone slain in the spirit on the floor in the church service, and someone from the pews, or a minister would come and touch that person.

They would touch them and this can hinder the spirit of God from dealing with them. This can hinder the spirit of God from healing and delivering that person who God is dealing with. The devil has his people too and they are in all the churches. Their mission is to try and hinder the move of God. That's why armor-bearers, prophets, or whosoever the Aaron(pastor): of the house has put in charge to be armor-bearer do exactly, as their pastor has told them. The main thing that your pastor will tell you is to watch, listen, look, and to observe everyone and everything at all times. If you don't watch, and listen with you natural eyes and ears how can you know what to pray for, or how can you listen unto the Holy Ghost within you to lead, guide, and to direct you. Armor-bearers are placed in the church to guard the anointing on the (pastor-head shepherd, Aarons): life. They are to watch and look for wolves in the churches that come in to divide, and to scatter the sheep. The armor-bearers are there to assist the pastor. They are there to lighten the load off of the pastor. They are there to make sure no one touches someone who is slain in the spirit. Prophets are mainly armor-bearers, as well, as deacons. They are all servants.

The problem is when the people of God inter-marry with nations that serve other Gods. For example a Christian should not marry someone who is of another religion. because when the two have children the one who is a Christian will have hell on their hands. The other spouse believes in another God and serve in a different religion. So what happens is that their children become confused, and they are taught about the Christian religion, and another religion, and this is defiance and disobedience unto God. God will not bless the couple, nor bless their children because of the inter-marrying. Now you can marry outside your race, but even if the person you desire to be your soul-mate make sure that you hear from God. Just because they say they are Christians and that their parents are Christians do not mean that they are from God. Remember that they could be lying to you. That's why we have all over the world especially in America so many divorces and messed up marriages, because of people of God marrying someone of another religion. This is also (witch-craft confusion): and therefore soul-ties will most likely be formed by marrying this person, and by having sexual intercourse with them. There are many (spiritual-witches): in the (churches): all over the world proclaiming to be of God. Having a form of Godliness, but denying the power thereof. The form of Godliness is that they come with all power and signs of God, but the lying-wonders is that they serve others Gods. Their motives are not good motives. The lying-wonders is that they deny the power of God. Just because they say that they believe in the power of God, and that they know, and love Jesus Christ does not mean that they are of God. They deny the power of God which is lying-wonders, because they present the word of God that they are from God. They (disguise, and camouflage): behind the word of God so that no one shall be able to know their true motives. But I'm here to tell you that in these last days God is exposing these false prophets, liars, seducers, manipulators, workers of iniquity, wolves in sheep clothing. many shall get sick and shall die. because these people are playing with the word of God. they are suing Gods word to deceive Gods people so that they may get unjust gain. the spiritual warfare is to get you to recognize that everything that you see and hear is not true. the only truth is God's word. The spiritual warfare is to let us know that we are not where we think we are at. It is to cause us to go forth in sacloth and ashes to come unto the threshing floor so that we may cry out to God in prayer. True spiritual warfare is to come to a point a (mastery: maturity): in the things of God. True spiritual warfare is to discern good from evil; to know who your enemy is, which is a spirit. For we wrestle not against flesh and blood, but against spirits. True spiritual warfare is to take the kingdom by force. Matthew Chapter 11: verse 12: And from the days of John the Baptist until now the kingdom of heaven suffereth violence, and the violent take it by force. The Kingdom of heaven is a place, and can be referred to the mind which is the high place, (the central head-quarters of operations). Peoples mind have been enslaved, bound, bewitched, seduced by the devil, and the (violent): which are the (true sons: and daughters: of God): take it by force. Take what by force? We take back the Kingdom of heaven, which is the minds of people back from the powers of darkness. The powers of darkness is witch-craft a tools that satan uses to camouflage jezebel. The apostle is a battle-ax: a warrior. Jehu in the book of 1st kings Chapter 19: verse 16: And Jehu the son of Nimshi shalt thou anoint to be king over Israel: and Elisha the son of Shaphat of Abelmeholah shalt thou anoint to be prophet in thy room. The anointing is Jehu was unlike no other anointing. Jehu's anointing was an anointing of an apostle. Even though the scripture says in 1st kings Chapter 19: verse 16: Thou shalt anoint to be prophet in thy room. What God was really saying that when he raises up apostles, which are the (master-builders), the (battle-ax): they are to confront (demonic-opposition). God anoint his apostles like Jehu to destroy jezebel, even though Jehu is old testament the symbolism is that the apostolic-anointing is very deadly. The prophets are the eyes, the ears, and the mouth-piece of God. They are the (watchman): of Gods sheep, which also includes the 5 fold ministers who are the apostles, the prophet, the pastor, the teachers, and the evangelist. The prophet acts like a bi- mental consultant unto the apostle. You see Jonathan was like the prophet and David was like the apostle. The prophets will confirm to the apostle the things which God have told them. Since the prophet operates mainly in intercession and spiritual warfare the prophet is to armor-bearer, watch, guard, and to protect the apostle. They are to pray over the (shepherd, pastor, Aaron): of the house of God. They are to do as the (pastor): says. They are to watch and cover the (pastor): at all times. God will a lot of times harden the hearts of the apostles to come against demonic-opposition(demonic- forces). Prophets come against demonic spirits. They come against demons. The apostle is to come against princes which are (fallen-angels): over (territories): Here is a prime example of a fallen-angel(prince). Daniel Chapter 10: verses 12-13: 12. Then said he unto me, fear not, Daniel: for from the first day that thou didst set thine heart to understand, and to chasten thyself before thy God, thy words were heard, and I am come for thy words. 13. But the prince of the kingdom of Persia withstood me one and twenty days: but, lo, Michael, one of the chief princes, came to help me; and I remained there with the kings of Persia. We see here that the prince of Persia was a man, but the (prince): (fallen-angel): was controlling the prince of Persia by the means of demons. Gabriel told Daniel that prayed and fasted for twenty one days that Michael the arch- angel has come to assist and to help. So the apostolic ministry is to build (functioning churches, businesses): to watch and oversee their churches. They are to make sure that the sheep are ok. The apostolic ministry is, and has been instituted to the body of Christ to battle (warfare): against the (powers: that be); which are the (fallen-angels) over (territories). In the book of Revelation Chapter 1: verse 10. I was in the spirit on the Lord's day, and heard behind me a great voice, as of a trumpet, the apostle has the uncanny ability like a seer to see in the spirit. Apostles can be seers. Seers can be apostles, some just called themselves seers even though they may in actuality be an apostle. Some just call themselves apostles even though they may in actuality be seers in disguise. The apostle is going to endure much more suffering that the prophet, pastor, teacher, and the evangelist because of the call of God on their life. Because of the purpose and assignment on their lives, the apostle are ones that are sent from God to do a special work for God. Apostles can hear directly from God just like John in verse 10 of Chapter 1 of revelation, also apostles have visions but their visions will be mainly apostolic-visions. Their vision will be to build Gods kingdom. Matthew Chapter 6: verse 10: thy kingdom come. Thy will be done in earth, as it is in heaven. God is a God of order and unity. In order for Gods kingdom to come down (manifest): in the earth-realm there must be apostles set in place who are called from God to build Gods kingdom. It's no different from Noah building the arch that God told him to build. Apostles will receive (blueprints): directly from God to build and to establish Gods kingdom.

What are the Signs: of a True-Apostle?

1. Romans Chapter 1: verse 1: Paul, a servant of Jesus Christ, called to be an apostle, separated unto the gospel of God, A true apostle of God must be separated. The fruit of a true apostle is their servant hood. True apostles of God have

seen and talked to Jesus one on one and face to face. 1st Corinthians Chapter 9: verse 1: Am I not an apostle? am I not free? have I not seen Jesus Christ our Lord? are not ye my work in the Lord?

2. 1st Corinthians Chapter 9:verse 2: If I be not an apostle unto others, yet doubtless I am to you: for the seal of mine apostleship are ye in the Lord. The sign of a true apostle is that they build, establish, watch over, and protect Gods sheep. Gods sheep is also the pastors that apostles have under them that are over their churches.

3. 2nd Corinthians Chapter 12: verse 12: Truly the signs of an apostle were wrought among you in all patience, in signs, and wonders, and mighty deeds. True apostles not only operate in all signs and wonders (miracles); but they have mighty deeds not of the flesh, but of the spirit: of God (fruit: of the spirit): Just because an apostle does not have a church, or churches already set in order and established does not mean that they are not apostles. Everything is patience and timing. Apostles mainly stay in the field though they are over churches and organizations. The Bishop which is an (Elder), or a more mature (Pastor/Apostle) is more of an in-house apostle. In-house mature, experienced Pastor (Elder).

4. Apostles are not man made, nor sent by man, but by God. Galatians Chapter 1: verse 1: Paul,

an apostle, (not of men, neither by man, but by Jesus Christ, and God the father, who raised him from the dead;)

5. 1st Timothy Chapter 2: verse 7: Whereunto I am ordained a preacher, and an apostle, (I speak the truth in Christ, and lie not;) a teacher of the gentiles in faith and verity. True apostles are seers. Not only can they prophesy but they operate exactly like a seer which can operate in the highest form of the prophetic-impartation. I said that not all Apostles are seers but all true apostles are seers. Everyone who says that they're an apostle is not an apostle. The Apostle Paul said not only is he a preacher (pastor, evangelist, teachers, prophet): but he's an apostle. The reason why he said that he was ordained as a preacher is because before you can become an (apostle): you must first be a (prophet). As I said before not ever prophet is a (seer–apostle), but every (apostle-seer): is a prophet. So the Apostle Paul is saying that he evangelized, he taught like a teacher (theologian), he pastured, he prophesied, and became an apostle. The Apostle Paul put in work. He was saying unto his son in the gospel timothy that there are different season in which God will take you through in order for the metamorphosis to occur.

6. 2nd Timothy Chapter 1: verse 11: Whereunto I am appointed a preacher, and an apostle, and a teacher of the gentiles. The main point is

that God will set his apostles in geographical-locations to set up, and establish churches and organizations. The Apostle Paul said that he is a teacher to the gentiles. Paul was not just an apostle (one who is send to build, set up, and to establishes churches, and organizations), but he says that he is appointed a preacher. A preacher is an (apostle, prophet, pastor, evangelist, or teacher). The apostle flows like a prophet. The apostle is the battle ax and the prophet is the sword. The apostles are (builders, they set things in order, build churches, organizations, protect their flock and sheep from wolves).

7. The apostle operates in all the gifts. 1st Corinthians Chapter 12: verse 4:

Chapter 11

The Office of the Prophet

The Office: of: a Prophet: Part 1:

What is a Prophet? A person who speak for god: by divine-inspiration: a spokesman of god. A person chosen by god: to lead: gods-people out of the wilderness, out of Egypt. Prophets: are the eyes, the ears and they are the mouthpiece: of: god. Prophets: of all the 5-fold-ministry: are the most mus-understood: of ll the fold: must protect the sheep: from wolves: to warn the people of judgement, and to speak, and declare the word: of: the lord. Hosea 12:13 And by a prophet: the lord: brought Israel out of Egypt, and by a prophet: was he preserved. The inner-circle: is the in-gathering: of: the prophets: which is old times, or old testament-times: called: seers: one who sees revelation, or can see into the spirit. 1 Samuel chapter 9: verse 9: Beforetime in Israel, when a man went to inquire of God, thus he spake, come, and let us go to the seer: for he that is now called a prophet: was beforetime called a seer. That's why the religious-system: of: the devil: don't want prophets; in their churches: because prophets: come to speak, and declare the word: of: the lord. And because prophets: are being ran off from the churches: destruction: comes upon them. A prophet: is one who has been called, chosen, ordained, and selected by god: to be gods-spokesman here on the earth. One that is the eyes, ears, and the mouthpiece of god. The prophet can see dreams and visions: numbers 12: 6-8 as, well, as hear the voice of god. A prophet: can bring forth judgment: as, well, as to proclaim blessings unto the people. The prophet: makes sense of all the chaos that is in your life and the potential: that one has to become all that god: has called: and chosen: for them to be. They can see beyond: the natural: and can connect: the world: of: the spirit: with the natural: by connecting worlds-together. They have the super-natural ability: to unlock peoples destiny.

The Office: of: a Prophet: Part 2: Developing, hearing and knowing the Voice of God:

The majority of all gods prophets have experienced god: speak to them earlier in their life, especially during their childhood in which god: was trying to get them familiar with his presence, as well, as his voice. Lets look at the book of 1st Samuel chapter 3: verses 4-21. We see that the lord: began to speak to Samuel: at such an early age until he was instructed by his father Eli: to answer the lord. In Isaiah chapter 65: verse 1: that i am sought of them that asked not for me; i am sought of them that asked not for me; i am found of them that sought me not; i said, behold me, behold me, unto a nation that was not called by my name. God sought you so you must seek him. But 1st of all you must be instructed: by mentors: to develop: you so that you can do greater- works: and be prepared: for the task, assignment, will, and purpose of god: for your life. Isaiah chapter 49: verse 23: states that's and kings shall be thy nursing fathers and their queens thy nursing mothers: they shall bow down and lick the dust of thy feet: and thy shalt know that i am the lord: for they shall not be ashamed that wait on me. You can never instruct, or lead unless you have been taught to lead. Bonus point: remember you cant give authority until you have been under authority: you are the protege: of your mentor and you can never leave to do the assignments that god has called and chosen for you to do unless your pastor or mentor gives you the authority to do so by the laying on of hands which is the transfer of the anointing. Or known, as the prophets-reward. You help and assist someone in their vision god will cause people to do the same for you and more. A.k.a. Inpartation. If you closely study the relationship between Elisha and Elijah: in 1st kings chapter 19: verses 19-21. Forsake everything and be subject to your authority: which is you man of woman of god. If you go against your authority you go against god. Ex 16:8 Moses tells the people that they are murmuring against him, but against god. 1st chronicles chapter 16: verse 22 states: touch not mine anointed and do my prophet no harm. Also in the book of psalms chapter 105: verse 15: it states that the same things which leads us to mark 3:29 that but he that shall blaspheme against the holy ghost: hath never forgiveness, but is in danger of eternal damnation. The word blaspheme: means to go against the word of god. To be disobedient. To be rebellious which is known as witchcraft. Turn to the book of 1t Samuel chapter 15: verse 24: and it states that for rebellion is as the sin of witchcraft: and stubbornness: is a iniquity and idolatry. Because thou hast rejected the word of the lord, he have also rejected thee from being king. Rebellion-resistance to authority; defiance against a government: through uprising or revolt. The word witchcraft: means the power: or practices: of a witch known, as sorcery. That's why Jesus states in the book of Matthew chapter 7: verses 21-23 that not everyone that saith unto me, lord, lord, shall enter into the kingdom:of: heaven, but he that doeth the will of my father which is in heaven. Many will say to me in that day, lord, lord, have we not prophesied in thy name? And in thy name have we cast out devils? And in thy name done many wonderful works? And then will i profess unto them depart from me, ye that work iniquity. They took gods words, principles, precepts, ordinances, commandments, statutes, and law because the word of god: has the power to produce; but they used it for their own selfish motives. Never misuse the power that god: has given you. 1st Corinthians 8: 9 but take heed lest this liberty of yours becomes a stumbling block to them that are weak. Your mentor is instructed on how to guide you on how to hear from god. When you go forth into prophecy you may say what if i feel like I'm saying the wrong thing? Then your mentor: or master prophet: which is your pastor: will instruct: you by the holy spirit: on what to do. If you say the wrong thing does it means that you're a false prophet? Absolutely not. You are false in what you said because of not having the prophet information from god. Bonus point: remember some things god gives you are not for no one to know but you and god. Remember somethings god gives you he want to to say, but it may not be time. Remember some things god gives you he wants you to say now. You just need move development. What if i prophesy and it does not come to pass? Am i a false prophet? Absolutely not. You may have said it out of order which means before time. You may have misunderstood what the spirit told you. You may have said part of what the spirit told you because of fear. What happens when i act in disobedience and give someone a prophecy? You give the devil an upper- hand. Matthew 7: 6 give not that which is holy unto the gods, neither cast ye your pearls before the swine, lest they trample them under their feet and turn again and rend you. In other word bonus point: the devil don't know no more than what you tell him. What is fear? To have faith in death, or a fear in failure. Because fear hath torment. The prophecy may not come to pass because of the persons disobedience to god: to follow through with the instruction of the cycle: of: manifestation. Which means that person missed their season. And remember in Seerology: which is a prophetic–group that i have that there are four season in which god will manifest. Just like there are 4 spirits: angels of the earth and god will and can manifest more that 4 seasons for you according to your obedience. In seerology: which is the science: of: the prophetic: prophets: they eyes, ears, and the mouthpiece: of god:

Seerology– prophecy: has a science, craft, skill, technique/ there is the discipline, and meditation of prophecy, there is a genesis: alpha, and omega of prophecy. There is the technology of prophecy.Universal prophecy– there is the government of prophecy, the law, purpose, and principles of prophecy,

history of prophecy– which is the culture of prophecy, th past, present, and the future of prophecy.

Compass of prophecy: which is the regions, territory, location, area, and atlas of prophecy: the geographical locations: of: prophetic events: and events; to come of the world. The prophetic economics: and prophetic wealth empowerment: of prophecy:

seasons– of prophecy: seasons to come, prophetic seasons of time, dates, and years.

The major prophets: and you have the minor prophets: the sacred: art: of: tongues: 1. Tongues: is a priestly ministry. 2. Tongues: is apostolic. 3. Stop speaking the worldly, stop cursing. 4. Speak as the oracle: which is the messenger of god: 5. Nationality: of; tongues: by speaking in different nationality of languages having never learned. 6. Tongues speaking: to god: the holy ghost: which is the holy spirit: speaking to god, praying to god: on your behalf.

Neophyte-greek: neos-a new convert 2. Convert- a new beginner, novice.

Minstrel: of: the prophet:-noun 1.A medieval poet and musician who sang or recited while accompanying himself on a stringed instrument, either as a member of a noble household or as an itinerant troubadour. 2.A musician, singer, or poet.

Minstrel: of: the prophet: instrument of the prophet: prophets are tuned into music, praise and worship. Like king David.

The psalmist: of the prophet: prophet: the sacred song, songs, of god, psaltery, tabret, pipe, harp. One who plays instrument: like prophet Kim clement:

4 season: 4 angels: of: the earth: 4 doors: of: opportunities open to gods people yearly. And can open more than that according to your faithfulness, and obedience unto God. Matthew 13:10-17 what is a parable? A parable is a dream in an image form. It is a dream in spoken-from. It is when god is trying to get your attention which is numbers chapter 12:

verse 6. Verse 7; dark-speeches. Dark-speeches: are dreams, riddles, proverbs, and parables. Mysteries: of: the kingdom; of: heaven: what are the mysteries: of: the kingdom; of: heaven? The mysteries: of: the kingdom; of: heaven: are keys:angels: like the group that i have called Angelology: to unlock destiny. What is destiny? Destiny: is the purpose that god: has called and chosen for you to do; and to fulfill. What is a key: a key: is an instrument: used to unlock peoples destiny. Say now out loud: that I'm a key: to unlocks peoples destiny. I am a door: to bless others. Others are keys: to unlock my untapped potential. Others are a door: for me to walk-in. So your jobs: prophets: seers: is to be a key: and a door: to unlock peoples destiny: and their potential. To that they may walk through the door. So if your prophecy don't line-up: by the word of God: it's of the devil. Bonus-point: don't prophecy: beyond the spirit: that is called divination: the foresight to see into the spirit without the spirit of god. Those who use divination are your psychics: who are not led by the spirit of god: but by demonic-influence. Matthew 7:15 do no i cast away the pearls with the swine? Absolutely not. Why? Because the wealth of the wicked is laid up for the just. The prophet: always have dreams and visions: yes, because they are visionaries: and they must be connected to the senior-pastor: which is the apostle: otherwise known as the Aaron:of: a church. Bonus- point: if you are called to be an apostle: you 1st will walk into the office of the prophet, then meta morphs into the apostolic. Proverbs 29:18 states that without a vision the people parish: but he that keepth the law happy is he. The prophets: stand at the gate; o fence- line: to warn, protect, and guide the people to safety. That why i have the group: called: battle-ax: watchman: at the gates: bonus-point: you kill the prophets: and the nations: gods-sheep are in danger of the wolves. And the wolves are going to kill the sheep. Prophets have been built to stand no matter the cost, nor price. The prophet: must hear with their spiritual-ear: and not their natural ear. We hear in the new testament: him that hath ears to hear let him hear what the spirit saith unto the churches, especially in the book of revelation. So in the book of numbers chapter 12: verse 7: it says: Moses my servant who is faithful in all my house with him will i speak mouth to mouth even apparently and not in dark speeches: say now: god speaks to me mouth to mouth or 1 to 1. You must use your time wisely and spend time with god always. God sometimes even at an early age speaks to his prophets in a loud audible-voice. But after a time god will start speaking to you in your spirit which is your soul, or soulish area. Say now: holy ghost: god: in me speak to me now. Guide me into all truth, bring all things back unto my remembrance that i need to know, and show and reveal to me things to come. John chapter 16: verse 13: in the book of Matthew 6: verses 5-6: go to your secret place: of prayer. What is the secret place? It's the secret place of the most high which is the apostolic. I talked about on blogtalkradio.com that with the apostolic and prophetic shift, mantels that the secret place is the apostolic. Its your time alone with god so god can suit your up with the proper-armor that you need. When does god reward you openly? Mk 11:24, 1st john 5:14-15. At the moment when you pray. In hearing the voice of god you will be tired, by test, trials, and tribulations. In order to mature and prefect your ability to hear and to discern the voice of god. It is more to it than just hearing the voice of god, because when you listen you get to understand. Because you must have a prayer-life: and prayer is communication with god and a relationship with god. Communicating with god, or communion with god. Because when you hear it goes out the other ear with no understanding that's why the bible says in Matthew 13: because they have no root they have joy for a moment but when persecution ariseth for the word sake they become offended and these are they that fall by the way-side. But when you listen to what god says with an understanding: prayer life: and you do what god tells you. You are thus declared a wise man, or a wise-master builder. Matthew 7: verse 24. Another way to hear from god and to tell if its from god is Jeremiah chapter 29: verse 11: for i know the thoughts that i think toward you, saith the lord, thoughts of peace, and not of evil, to give you a good and expected end. You can test prophecy by exhortation, edification, comfort, if its of good and of peace. Also prophecy can be warnings and it does not mean its from the devil. In other messages we will also be dealing with dream and vision interpretation.

Developing, hearing and knowing the Voice: of: God: Hearing: from God:

What is discernment? Discern means to distinguish between the good and evil. Right and wrong. Which leads us to the spirit of discernment? To get an understanding of what spirit you are entertaining: whether it is of god, or the devil. In the spirit of discernment: the lord: will allow you to see what spirit is on a person: whether it is of god, or the devil. But do not cast the demonic-spirit: out of the person unless the lord: tells you too lest they turn and rend you. Let's look at the book of acts chapter 19: verses 13-17. Now we see the vagabond Jews: exorcists: and the 7 sons of sceva, a Jew who tries to rebuke a devil out of a man and the devil told the man Jesus i know, Paul i know, but who are you. And the devil whipped: the men out of their clothes. You can also get whipped out of your spiritual clothes also. Meditation: you must meditate: on the word: of; god: daily. That's why Joshua chapter 1 verse 8: says, this book of the law shall not depart out of thy mouth, but thou shalt meditate on it day and night that thou mayest observe to do according as it is written. For then thou shalt make thy way prosperous and then thou shalt have good success. The book of the law: was referred: to as the Pentateuch: which are the 5 books of Moses: and that's all Joshua: had at that time. We have no book of the law but we have the holy ghost. Which means no book of the law. A lot of things are missing out of the bible so the holy spirit which is the holy ghost has it all. That's why the bible says in john chapter 16: verse 13 that the holy spirit: will guide us into all truth and bring all things back unto our remembrance. Turn to the book of Matthew chapter 22: verses 36-40. In the book of john chapter 16; verse 13: it states; that howbeit when he, the spirit of truth is come he will guide you into all truth: for he shall nor speak of himself; but whatsoever he shall hear that shall he speak; and he will show you things to come. The holy ghost: is the law and the prophets: that's why the bible says in 2 Corinthians 3:6: that for the letter killeth, but the spirit giveth life. You can read the bible from genesis to revelations, but without a relationship with god you can easily become a tool of the devil. Knowing the bible is great but do you have a relationship with god: through Jesus Christ. Remember Jesus said in the book of john chapter 10: that he is the door all that ever came before him were thieves and robbers. No man can come to the father unless they come through him. Because the devil; knows the bible and he has his ministers, workers: the gates; of: hell: which are witches, and warlocks; workers of iniquity: ready lying in wait to deceive you. As stated in the book of 2 Corinthians chapter 11: verses 13-15 to not be alarmed when you see false prophets. Those whose motives are wrong and not for god. Why because they are only these as opposition against you that that god: can get his glory. Bonus point: a lot of people say they don't go to church because of hypocrites: which are false people: but god: allow the tares to be in the churches with the wheat to get you ready for the world. If you not faithful over 1 devil how can god bless you with more blessings on the other side with more devil. Bonus point: the same faith it takes you to get something from god is the same faith its going to take you to keep it. Because the devil is coming to see if you know who you are. Be thankful that they are coming against you why? Because god brought them your way in order for them to see how a real prophet is suppose to operate. Also when a false prophet: is against you thank god that they are not deceiving others, but if you allow the spirit to speak to you, then you will not be alarmed, or scared when negative and evil occurrences come in your life. You must understand the prophet signs: and symbols: that God has places with and around you, lest you will cast out the pearls with the swine. A lot of times god is trying to bless us and we think it's the devil and we break and run. Yes prophets are bi-polar and ski-to: schizophrenia: bonus-point: prophets see demons and have experienced; demons from childhood. And the prophecy becomes a lie because we did not stand on what god promised us. Why did you think Jesus said in the book of mark chapter 11: verse 22: that have faith in god. Not in your ability, nor others ability but in god-ability: which is the word of god. What God told you and promised you, because he want to talk to you in the process of your storm. Bonus- point: like a preacher once told me watch, listen, look, and observe: why? Because if you're not watching you want know what to pray about. That why we have so many undeveloped

Christians, ministers and especially prophets: who are cheating the process of their development. That why in the wilderness is the best place for a prophet: so that god: may tear them down and build them back up properly. So a lot of prophets who are being labeled: as a false prophet: are in actuality being over persecuted because they are out of order, or out of the system. The apostle Paul: stated: that in the book of 1st Corinthians chapter 14: verse 33: that for god is not the author of confusion, but of peace, as in all churches of the saints. Everyone say now that i walk in the peace of god. I have peace with god and god has peace with me. Say now i follow the order of god. The 1st step to walking here on earth, as a prophet of God is that you must hear the voice of god which must be developed: as you go through trials, tests, and tribulations.

Isolation: Volume 3: Silence: of the Prophets:

There is a trying season in every prophets life where they will be put to silence. This is a season of testing to groom the prophets in mastery. Prophets love to talk even though seers are prophets. But not every prophet is a seer. The prophets have and walk in a government-anointing: as found in the book of Zechariah chapter 3: verses 6–10: and in the book of Isaiah chapter 22: verses 19–25: prophets will mainly walk in a government-anointing in the local churches and in local places. Your seers will mainly walk in a government-anointing in greater-depths and in greater dimensions of the prophetic-inpartation that the prophet. The seers will be in very great high places giving direction unto governments, and leaders. God will train the prophets to be alone to develop them in the fruit of the spirit, in the character of Christ. To build them to stand against the opposition of the devil. God will allow the prophets to be in years of silence and when god is ready god will elevate them. And he will give them a platform to declare the power and presence of god. A lot of pastors are really apostles but they chose not to go under that name because of the onslaught of the devil. So do not care about the warfare of the devil. Many prophets are bi-polar and schizophrenic because God chose the foolish things to confound the wise. God will use a nobody and make them somebody. Because of the words that comes out of the prophets mouth god will cause their gift to make room for them. And bring them before great men and women. The silence: of the prophets: is a time of testing. The wilderness-experience: where the prophet: experiences: god one on one. Like when Moses met god as stated in the book of exodus chapter 3. These trying times for the prophets of god is to mold and to shape them into mastery. When to speak and when not to speak. God must try his servants the apostles, prophets, pastors, teachers, evangelists his servants which are prophets messengers of god. But the one born to declare gods word. To see into the realm of the spirit. To be the mouthpiece of god is the prophet. God will develop his servant the prophet in places that others would not go. True prophets of god confront demonic-opposition that comes from the spirit: of Jezebel. Which Jezebel tries to hi-jack the prophetic-ministry. The stream in which the prophet operates in is mainly verbal and the seer mainly operates in the visionary states. Seers are prophets. But no all prophets are seers. People will think that the prophets are crazy, but they are not. They are crazy in the sense of peculiar, strange, mystical, and unusual. God in these last days is revealing the ministry of the prophet: the watchman: in many multiple streams like never before. God will try the prophets as for as their faith in obedience. God will try the prophets to declare and to deliver the word of the lord. God will try the prophet to trust in him and no one else. God will try the prophet with people to develop them in the spirit: of discernment. God will try the prophet to walk alone. God will try the prophet to create from within themselves. Prophets carry a creative-anointing: to speak things into existence. God will try the prophet: with his word to develop them in mastery. God is raising up prophets in every mostly every profession around the world to be a witness of the lord Jesus Christ before the end comes. Prophets turn the hearts of the fathers to the children. And the hearts of the children to their fathers lest god come and smite the earth with a curse.

Chapter 12

Masterprophet

A master prophet is an apostle, even though the word master prophet is not found in the bible we are to seek the spirit. Its' not about names, nor titles, but Jesus said that in the book of John Chapter 13: verse 35: By this shall all men know that ye are my disciples, if ye have love one to another. The sign that they are from God Is that they walk in love. They not only say and speak as the oracles of Christ their whole lifestyle Is a lifestyle of servant hood. Even the word master-teacher unto many may seem blasphemous unto them, but it does not matter what others think. The only voice that should matter is Gods word. The bible is foundational but there are many things and many books that have been removed out of the bible throughout the ages. That's why Jesus states' in the book of John Chapter 16: verse 13: that the Holy Spirit will guide us into all truth not facts but into all truth, which means that as Colossians Chapter 1: verse 16: states: For by him were all things created, that are in heaven, and that are in earth, visible and invisible, whether they be thrones, or dominions, or principalities, or powers: all things were created by him, and for him:

So many people get caught up in gossip by slandering someone's name, or title but as believers in Christ (Christians): we are not suppose to do that. The bible is just foundational. We are to seek God for the revelation of what the word of God is actually saying. So what if people call themselves master prophet, master-teacher, or Arch bishop? Its' not our job to judge by condemning one another. A house divided against itself cannot stand. We are to judge by the spirit of discernment because if they are walking in titles, clergy names, and in positions that God never gave them then they are going to fall indeed. When we see our brother fall we are to help them get back up on course. Jesus said that you shall know them by their fruits. The word master prophet is a name of an apostle, elder, bishop; those who are very mature in the things of God. Just like the name master-teacher. it's the name of an apostle, elder, or bishop. Even though there are many pastors, evangelists, and teachers who are really elders, bishops, prophets, and apostles in disguise. Some of them do not want to be known as that because of the persecution that comes with those titles. Some do not care about the persecution that comes with the titles they just choose not to go by those titles because of all of the chaos that has happened throughout the ages. Ephesians Chapter 6: verse 9: And, ye masters, do the same things unto them, forbearing threatening: knowing that your Master also is in heaven; neither is there respect of persons with him. Colossians Chapter 4: verse 1: Masters, give unto your servants that which is just and equal; knowing that ye also have a Master in heaven. These scriptures are not saying that we are God the father, nor is it saying that we are God almighty. What the scriptures are saying is that those in leadership are like masters mature people in leadership who govern over others. Its' just like a man, his wife, and kids that the husband is the head and he is like the master because Christ ordained the husband as the head of the household. It is the leaders job just like it is the husbands job to teach his family the word of God to be the provider and the protector of the family. So the pastor, elder, bishop, the apostle over the house of God is like a master one who is like an elder more experienced in the things of God. 1st Timothy Chapter 3: verses 1-7: 1. This is a true saying, if a man desires the office of a bishop, he desireth a good work. 2. A bishop then must be blameless, the husband of one wife, vigilant, sober, or good behavior, given to hospitality, apt to teach; 3. Not given to wine, no striker, not greedy of filthy lucre; but patient, not a brawler, not covetous; 4. One that ruleth his own house, having his children in subjection with all gravity; 5. (for if a man know not how to rule his own house, how shall he take care of the church of God?) 6. not a novice, lest being lifted up with pride he fall into the condemnation of the devil. 7. Moreover he must have a good report of them which are without; lest he fall into reproach and the snare of the devil.

I used 1st timothy Chapter 3: verses 1-7: as an example to show you about masters. It's the word mastery which is a noun which means victory; authority. Mastery is to mature us in the character and things of Christ. We are all given authority over the earth. We are given authority and responsibility to rule over something. Not everyone is called to be a leader especially if you are a pastor or one who is over the house of God. Ezekiel Chapter 3: verses 17-21: 17. Son of man, I have made thee a watchman unto the house of Israel: therefore hear the word at my mouth, and give them warning from me. 18. When I say unto the wicked, thou shalt surely die; and thou givest him not warning, nor speakest to warn the wicked from his wicked way, to save his life; the same wicked man shall die in his iniquity; but his blood will I require at thine hand. 19. Yet if thou warn the wicked, and he turn not from his wickedness, nor from his wicked way, he shall die in his iniquity; but thou hast delivered thy soul. 20. Again, when a righteous man doth turn from his righteousness, and commit iniquity, and I lay a stumbling block before him, he shall die; because thou hast not given him warning, he shall die in his sin, and his righteousness which he hath done shall not be remembered; but his blood will I require at thine hand. 21. Nevertheless if thou warn the righteous man, that the righteous sin not, and he doth not sin, he shall surely live, because he is warned; also thou hast delivered thy soul. I used Ezekiel Chapter 3: verses 17-21: as a reference about masters which is leadership. You have just read through the scriptures about God instructing the apostle Ezekiel that God was instructing and giving warning unto him. When are given a mandate to be in authority this is very serious and you shall be responsible for Gods people. The bible gives very clear instructions and warnings about abusing your authority, and abusing Gods people. In the book of 1st Corinthians Chapter 13: verse 11: When I was a child, I spake as a child, I understood as a child, I thought as a child: but when I became a man, I put away childish things. This scripture is talking about maturity. Part of your maturity in Christ is to let the past go. Letting the past go can be a painful thing. Letting go of people who mean you no good. I remember when I was a prophet how people would just come to me all the time and call me all the time for a word from the Lord. I did not know that I was a lot of times operating in divination which is the foresight to see going beyond the spirit. The Holy Spirit told me one day what I was doing and that the people who I thought loved me were really using me for selfish gain. They didn't love me, nor care about me. It was hard for me to let them go, but the Lord hardened my heart to leave them alone. This was a developmental stage for me that I had mastered. Philippians Chapter 3: verse 13: brethren, I count not myself to have apprehended: but this one thing I do, forgetting those things which are behind, and reaching forth unto those things which are before.

God will place people in your life to mature you. And one of the hard lessons if life is to forgive people for what they have done unto you. God will allow you to go through the same thing until you can master your mountain. This book dreams and visions volume I: is just the preface to many of the other books that will follow after this book that you are reading now. There are many diverse mysteries within the word of God but they are hidden in the spirit. Once I began to hear the Lords voice in 2001 all hell broke loose in my life.

Key Point # 61:
The religious-system of the devil composed of Scribes, Pharisees, and Saduccess do not care if you serve or clean in the church. They don't have a problem with you tithing, sowing seeds, or giving first fruits. They don't have a problem with what you do. They have a problem with who you have become. It's all about becoming the person that God desires for you to be. God will place you under false-prophets while you are a babe in the Lord, then when you start to grow in maturity God will branch you out from among them because of your maturity. The religious system doesn't want anyone to serve God in the church, but them. That's why Jesus said in the book of Matthew Chapter 23: verse 16, 24: Woe unto you, ye blind guides, which say, whosoever shall swear by the temple, it is nothing; but whosoever shall swear by the gold of the temple, he is a debtor! 24. Ye blind guides, which strain at a gnat, and swallow a camel. Which means they can master the mysteries of God and the law, but they can't understand the love of God grace, mercy, and forgiveness. Our jobs' as saints of

God is to forgive them and to move forward no matter what. I look forward to seeing you in my other volumes. I can be reached @ christophercovingtonministries@outlook.com 713.817.7774 dynasty7ministries.com